Harbors of Hope

The Planning for School and Student Success Process

Wayne Hulley
Linda Dier

304 West Kirkwood Avenue
Bloomington, Indiana 47404-5132
(812) 336-7700
(800) 733-6786 (toll free)
FAX: (812) 336-7790
e-mail: nes@nesonline.com
www.nesonline.com

Cover design by Grannan Graphic Design, Ltd.
Text design by T.G. Design Group

Printed in the United States of America

ISBN: 1-932127-44-5

Dedication

To all school staff members who work to inspire hope and create positive futures for students.

Table of Contents

About the Authors
Wayne Hulley and Linda Dier vii

Foreword
Effective, Efficient, and Excellent ix

Introduction
Creating Harbors of Hope 1

PART 1 Harbors of Hope:
Schools With Character and Competence 5

Chapter 1
Harbors of Hope: Three Schools That
Lead the Way 7

Chapter 2
Harbors of Hope: What We Have Learned 39

Chapter 3
Harbors of Hope: A Proven Approach 57

PART 2 Strategies for Creating Harbors of Hope 67

Chapter 4
Plan to Improve: Who Is in Charge? 69

Chapter 5
Set the Course (Values, Vision, Purpose) 81

Chapter 6
Study 89

Chapter 7
Reflect 101

Chapter 8
Plan 121

Chapter 9
High-Yield Strategies: Keys to Goal Attainment ... 137

Chapter 10
Implement 169

Chapter 11
Creating the Culture for Change 181

Chapter 12
Building on Success: Continuous Improvement ... 197

PART 3 Appendix 205
Thirteen Brain-Activating Strategies 207

References 213

About the Authors

Wayne Hulley and Linda Dier

Wayne Hulley, B.A., M.Ed., M.A., is the president of Canadian Effective Schools Inc. in Burlington, Ontario. He has been a teacher, a principal, and a superintendent in and around the Toronto area. His work in school improvement has spanned 35 years and has allowed him to work in schools and school districts throughout North America. He has taught motivational theory at three major universities and is a senior consultant with the FranklinCovey Company. In partnership with National Educational Service, he offers workshops, seminars, and institutes on effective schools and school improvement. Wayne can be contacted at canadianeffectiveschools @sympatico.ca.

Linda Dier, B.A., B.Ed., M.Ed., is affiliated with Canadian Effective Schools Inc. as a senior consultant and administrator of the Canadian Effective Schools League. Her career in education spans over 30 years, during which time she worked in Saskatchewan and Manitoba as a classroom teacher (K–12), music specialist, school counselor, and administrator. During her time in administration, she worked as vice-principal, principal, and assistant superintendent. She has taught courses at the University of Manitoba and is a partner with LDG Consulting Group. Linda offers workshops and facilitates training to support planning for school and student success. She can be contacted at canadianeffectiveschools@shaw.ca or ldier@shaw.ca.

Foreword

Effective, Efficient, and Excellent

School reform efforts in the United States and Canada have much in common. Generally speaking, the call for reform has been initiated by policy makers at the provincial or federal level and has taken the form of top-down, mandate-driven requirements that describe the outcomes schools are expected to produce. The need to reform the school systems of both countries is compelling as we get further and further into the high-technology information age. The problem with most reform initiatives, however, is that they tell the local school leaders what is expected by way of results but are silent on how best to achieve those results. Nor do they explain how to effectively manage changes made to the system in place. What local educators are desperately seeking is a "theory of action" for how to best respond to the calls for reform.

Such a theory of action can be found in the book you are holding. *Harbors of Hope: The Planning for School and Student Success Process,* by Wayne Hulley and Linda Dier, offers a proven and practical process to guide the action of individual schools.

The case studies presented by the authors provide clear evidence that educators can make a sustainable difference in schools if they are committed to the vision and values associated with "Learning for All—Whatever It Takes." The process described by Hulley and Dier works and can be effectively managed in any and every school.

The underlying framework for this book is based on the lessons learned over the past quarter century in the Effective Schools Research. I have been privileged to be associated with that research and the resulting theory of action for most of that time. I know that teachers and school administrators are good people trying to do well on behalf of the students they attempt to serve. I know that most of them are doing the best they know how to do given the systems and circumstances in which they find themselves. I know that, given the right conditions and reasonable levels of support and encouragement, most would modify their professional practices if they became convinced it would benefit the students. If teachers and school leaders use the wisdom and guidance provided in this book, good things will happen for children.

Three critical terms help to support the rationale for this book and the approach to school improvement that it offers. The term "effective" has been defined as doing the right thing. The authors begin by asking the school community to come to a deep understanding of their core purpose and core values. "Efficient" has been defined as doing the right thing in the right way. Alignment of the curriculum and the instructional practices, as recommended in the book, will assure that the system will be both effective and efficient. The third term that is often heard,

and probably overused, is "excellent." "Excellent" can be defined as doing the right thing in the right way, and better than most.

Schools that qualify, by the authors' standards, as Harbors of Hope can also claim to be effective, efficient, and excellent schools, simultaneously. Committed educators can learn a great deal from studying these Harbors of Hope and the strategies that guided their journeys. One of the sources of hope for me—and perhaps for you as well—is that each school can become a Harbor of Hope if the adults who serve that school choose to make it so.

—Lawrence W. Lezotte
Effective Schools Products, Ltd.
Okemos, Michigan

Introduction

Creating Harbors of Hope

Although school improvement, or reform, has a long history, most of the initiatives from the "Excellence Movement" of the mid-1980s through the "Restructuring" of the mid-1990s have failed to produce the desired changes. This is not because they were badly conceived but because they failed to take into account the complexity of human dynamics within the educational system. Today, political influences, high-stakes testing, and budget restraints have placed added pressures on school systems and increased the demands for change.

What most earlier reform movements shared was an emphasis on the cognitive, the rational, the theoretical. What our experiences have taught us, though, is that the emotional component of school improvement must not be neglected. It is our belief that school improvement is as much an act of the heart as it is an act of the head. The schools we have seen that have achieved success and become effective are called "Harbors of Hope" for a reason: they emphasize hope, and they are willing to undertake not just restructuring but what we call reculturing to reach their goals.

Effective schools research, conducted over a 30-year period, has proven repeatedly that schools can, in fact, control enough variables to ensure that all students learn and function well in school. The research shows that schools where children know that they are safe and can achieve success see improved behavior, attitudes, and attendance. Effective schools actively plan for continuous school improvement and subscribe to the mission of "Learning for All—Whatever It Takes."

Schools that make a difference for all children are wonderful places where hope fuels all activity and futures are created. They combine strong character with strong competence to provide conditions and support to ensure that all students learn and are successful in school. Fullan (1993) contends that technical planning has not worked in educational change and that political pressures have failed to make a difference. He suggests that innovation should be built on a deeper understanding of the complex interrelationship of emotion, hope, empathy, and shared purpose. True school reform requires shared hope and passion.

Hope is a powerful emotion. Hope for a better future is often the thing that keeps people going in the face of incredible odds. Hope is a form of optimism that often seems unwarranted. It is the incentive that keeps people "keeping on." In the school context, hope is the belief that all students can learn and that school staffs are capable of turning that belief into a reality.

We envision the school improvement process as a journey to be undertaken by people who are highly motivated and passionately committed to working at giving and sustaining hope for all members of the community. We envision collaborative teams with shared values united in creating a safe place where

plans can be made and improvement strategies implemented within an atmosphere of support and protection. We think of these schools as Harbors of Hope, and we think of the process of planned improvement as a series of exciting adventures along the way.

The journey of school improvement has the potential to lead us into uncharted waters where storms of controversy may rage and conditions can be difficult. Harbors of Hope are inhabited by passionate people who are inspired by hope and the desire to make a difference. They are places where staff are supported and feel safe to implement new ideas that will make a difference for all students as they navigate the school improvement journey.

In the first chapter of this book we share the stories of exciting schools we have known that qualify in our estimation as Harbors of Hope. These schools all exhibit remarkable levels of character and competence and have significantly impacted students and their learning. Each of the schools is quite distinct; however, we believe that they also share some common characteristics. Our aim is to borrow from their examples as we describe processes that can be used to create Harbors of Hope wherever sufficient passion will fuel efforts at reculturing. Subsequent chapters of this book focus on the skills and processes required to enhance school and student success.

We have drawn upon the work of colleagues who are recognized as leaders in education, as well as upon our own observations and experiences. At all times we are sustained by the words of the late Ron Edmonds (1982), who wrote that

> . . . we can, wherever and whenever we choose, successfully teach all children whose schooling is of interest to

> us. We already know more than we need to do that. Whether or not we do it must finally depend on how we feel about the fact that we haven't so far. (p. 11)

We believe that teachers care about their work with children. This book affirms school improvement efforts that have been made thus far. It will also help you plan for the future with greater understanding of what is required for sustained school improvement, and it will arm you with the skills and structures to achieve it.

We cannot direct the winds but we can adjust our sails. We invite you to embark on a journey toward creating your own Harbor of Hope.

—Wayne Hulley and Linda Dier

Part 1

Harbors of Hope:

Schools With Character and Competence

Chapter 1

Harbors of Hope: Three Schools That Lead the Way

When preparing to write this book, we decided to focus on practical plans and actions that lead to improved learning outcomes for all students. Rather than begin by quoting research findings, we decided to share real examples of schools that we would consider to be Harbors of Hope. Sacred Heart Community School in Regina serves children in an inner-city area on the Saskatchewan prairies. With clear vision and staff commitment, this elementary school significantly improved learning outcomes for students and gave them hope for success in their educational futures. Lawrence Heights Middle School in Toronto also had a history of low performance and behavioral concerns. Through the introduction of carefully planned activities, the staff was able to positively impact all students. Monticello High School in Charlottesville, Virginia, was opened in 1998 and had difficulty attracting students because parents feared it would fail to match the performance of other schools in the district. The staff promised their community academic success and over a 2-year period did what was required to keep that promise. We consider these schools to be Harbors of Hope and have provided more in-depth information about them in the sections that follow.

Sacred Heart Community School: A Saskatchewan Harbor of Hope

In 1994, when Loretta Tetrault became principal of Sacred Heart Community School, she embarked on a journey that not even she could have anticipated. Sacred Heart is an inner-city school in Regina, Saskatchewan, that serves 350 students from pre-kindergarten to grade eight. The majority of students there live in poverty, and over 60% of them are of aboriginal heritage. The transient rate exceeds 30% annually. When Loretta took over, performance levels on provincial tests were falling two grade-equivalent years behind average. Suspensions had increased to 127 full days per year and the incidence of violence was very high. Relationships between students, teachers, and parents were characterized by frustration and blame. The school was in crisis.

Loretta found a discouraged staff that cared deeply about students but had lost hope of being able to do anything that would make a difference in these children's lives. She knew that one of the first things she needed to do was work with her staff to rekindle their confidence in themselves as teachers. She needed also to convince them that they could not allow difficult community and family influences to discourage their efforts on behalf of their students. Together, all at Sacred Heart were about to embark on a truly noteworthy journey of school reculturing.

Although Loretta was the principal of Sacred Heart when school improvement initiatives were begun, she credits the staff

with the ultimate success they achieved. "I will take the credit for initiating the change," she allows, but she points out that "the 'I' very quickly became 'we' when the results of some of our efforts started to show" (Effective Schools League, 2004).

Renewal From the Inside Out

Together, Loretta and her staff recognized that they would have to do things differently than they had in the past if they were to have a positive impact on student performance and behavior in their school. They concluded that if they were to be successful, they would have to eliminate teacher isolation and become team players. To begin, they studied the seven correlates of effective schools identified by Lawrence Lezotte and his associates (see below), and they chose to focus their initial efforts on two of the correlates: the creation of a "safe and orderly environment" and a "climate of high expectations for success." They also began to explore the research on brain-based learning, learning styles, multiple intelligence, emotional intelligence, differentiated instruction, and the effects of poverty.

The Seven Correlates of Effective Schools

1. Instructional leadership
2. Clear and focused mission
3. Safe and orderly environment
4. Climate of high expectations for success
5. Frequent monitoring of student progress
6. Positive home-school relations
7. Opportunity to learn and time on task

Together, the staff committed to the creation of a warm, loving atmosphere where students could take pride in their culture while accepting responsibility for their behavior and learning. The staff's stated quest was to provide a safe and orderly environment and to improve the academic performance of their students, most of whom lived in poverty. Sacred Heart began its journey to becoming a Harbor of Hope by developing a school Responsibility Plan. The plan was founded on the staff's commitment to treating every student with dignity and respect while working to establish a climate of safety and order. At the same time, the staff began to focus on ways of acknowledging positive efforts in order to reinforce positive choices.

Actions Leading to Success

1995–1996: Responsibility Plan Goals

1. Treat every student with dignity and respect:
   - Use in-school suspensions instead of out-of-school suspensions.
   - Establish a quiet room for reflecting and teaching.
2. Acknowledge positive efforts:
   - Implement a "caught being a positive role model" system.
   - Set weekly classroom goals.
   - Create attendance, attitude, and academic (AAA) awards.

Thinking Outside of the Box

As the Sacred Heart Staff built their collaborative culture, they found themselves thinking creatively about issues they

faced in their school. For example, during the previous year, the staff had struggled with a group of grade five students they referred to as "the class from hell." This group of very energetic children had a lot of leadership ability and no legitimate way of using it. After considerable deliberation and discussion, the staff agreed to establish two unique class configurations that would have these students, now in grade six, work with grade two students. Their theory was that placing the grade six students in leadership positions and expecting them to be role models for the grade two students would harness and direct their energies. The plan worked beautifully, and by the end of the year, "the class from hell" had earned a new nickname: "the holy ghosts." Since that first trial, this strategy has become so firmly embedded in the school culture that today all classes except kindergarten are uniquely combined.

As the staff implemented their Responsibility Plan and refined their unique grade combinations, they found that their efforts were beginning to be rewarded during class time; however, unstructured times like before and after school, as well as recess and noon hour, were still problematic. Sacred Heart students often got into conflicts with students from neighboring schools while going to and from school. Recess and noon hour were also times when a lot of misbehavior still occurred. During those times, students fell back into old behaviors that were of concern. Reculturing had to be more comprehensive, it seemed. After conducting conversations with students, the staff devised a plan to alter the school day to eliminate the problem times. The plan created a simple school day of morning classes, a half-hour lunch break, and afternoon classes. The proposal to alter the school day was referred to the central office and the senior administrators won approval for it from the provincial government. The stage was set.

In the revised plan, students no longer had a scheduled recess time. The staff realized that students needed positive outlets for expending their energy. They also knew that if their students could release pent-up energy and increase their fitness levels, they would be able to learn more effectively. Thus each class was scheduled for two physical education periods each day: one in the gym and one outdoors. Carefully planned activities focused on building the skills of teamwork and practicing the discipline of following basic rules. Students were also encouraged to remain at school for the half-hour lunch break. Almost all of them did. Support staff and parents supervised them during that time, providing games and activities for students once they had eaten.

With values and structures in place to support a safe and orderly learning environment, the Sacred Heart staff was able to focus its efforts on student achievement. Their research led them to conclude that it was time to revamp their Learning Resource Program in order to move away from the pull-out model previously used. The fact was that most students in the school were functioning well below grade level and a plan was needed that would enable staff to observe and track the progress of all children. Early intervention plans were developed for students in kindergarten through third grade. In-class direct support through co-planning and team teaching became the norm at the middle years (grades four through eight). These changes to the Learning Resource Program quickly resulted in improved student attitudes and achievement. Teachers moved away from textbook learning and toward resource and interest-based learning. This made a big difference to the students, and the teachers began to see positive outcomes for their efforts. When that happened, nothing could hold the teachers back from continuing their school improvement efforts.

Collaboration for School and Student Success

As the staff of Sacred Heart turned their attention to learning and student achievement, they studied Howard Gardner's theory of multiple intelligences and that of Eric Jensen on brain-based learning. Leadership in these areas was shared when a team of four teachers joined the administration to attend a 5-day Accelerated Learning Conference about brain-based learning with the understanding that over the next 2 years they would share their expertise in this area with their colleagues.

Actions Leading to Success

1996–1997

- Creation of unique grade combinations
- Permission sought to restructure day to provide more structured time and adult support
- Revamping of Learning Resource Program
- Shift of focus to learning and to incorporating the work of Howard Gardner and Eric Jensen

1997–1998

- Implementation of revised school day
- Staff development for differentiated instruction using multiple intelligences, accelerated learning, multi-age instruction, and teaching for emotional intelligence

In the spring of 1998 the staff applied for and received a grant from the Dr. Stirling McDowell Foundation for Research into Teaching. The grant would allow them to extend the work they had already begun. They called this new phase Project X (Excellence).

The grant money allowed the staff of Sacred Heart to do things they had only dreamed of prior to that. Now, along with continued professional development, rich opportunities were created for teacher collaboration. All teachers were teamed with partners at or near the same grade level. Additionally, all became members of a larger team that would collaborate to develop thematic units and special learning activities. Common preparation times were scheduled and teachers were provided with release time to visit each other's classrooms. Teaching partners set up their timetables to allow for team teaching or flexible student groupings to better meet individual needs. Instruction was adapted to build on what was known about the developmental stages, interests, and abilities of their students. As instructional practice changed, so did evaluation strategies. Soon rubrics and portfolios became standard at Sacred Heart, allowing students to know what was expected of them, thus enabling them to participate in the evaluation of their own performance.

The support that teachers provided to each other resulted in a positive energy that gathered momentum. Bi-weekly professional development meetings were established at which staff teams made presentations to each other about new insights and their work with children. Teachers came to understand and appreciate each other's strengths and gifts as teachers. A synergy developed that was evident throughout the school. The staff of Sacred Heart was working as a professional learning community in various configurations and the positive outcomes were significant.

The staff of Sacred Heart soon recognized the need to collect data on student learning in order to determine whether their efforts were, in fact, improving achievement levels. In Regina, the Canadian Achievement Tests (CAT) are administered annually

Actions Leading to Success

1998–1999

- Project X is born.
- Testing process is implemented to collect critical evidence in reading and language.
- Extensive staff development is underway.
- Professional learning communities with support structures are established.

1999–2000

- Project X enters phase 2.
- Use of critical evidence to track student growth becomes standard practice.
- Brain Activating Oasis is established (13 brain-activating strategies).

2000–2001

- Project X enters phase 3.
- Staff has become data-hungry.
- Proficiency targets are created.
- Consistent mental models are established.

at grades four and seven. The staff of Sacred Heart concluded that data yielded by these tests did not reflect student learning at Sacred Heart because of the transience in that population. In view of this, the school decided to embark on an annual baseline testing process using the literacy sub-sections of the Canadian Tests of Basic Skills (CTBS) with all students. Using this instrument with all students enables the determination of each one's grade equivalent levels in the three areas twice a year: in October and again in May. The information gathered through this testing process has allowed staff to address individual learning needs as well as assess overall school growth.

Having successfully used their first grant, the staff at Sacred Heart received a second grant from the Dr. Stirling McDowell Foundation and agreed that the next step in their journey of improvement would be to create a "Brain Activating Oasis" at Sacred Heart where individual learning would be the main focus. The staff identified 13 brain-activating strategies and techniques to use in the oasis. The unanimous adoption of this plan by the staff created an instructional alignment in the school that has allowed teachers to build on each other's work from year to year.

Sacred Heart's 13 Brain-Activating Strategies

- Changing from teaching to "activating brains"
- Incidental learning: the little things are the big things
- Stimulating environment
- Hallway huddles
- Learning states
- Music
- Brain breaks
- Real math
- Eye patterns and thinking
- Daily oral language
- Mind mapping/concept webbing
- Assessment
- Our Catholic faith

Descriptions of each strategy are provided in the appendix on page 207.

When the staff of Sacred Heart received a third grant from the Dr. Stirling McDowell Foundation for Research into Teaching, they decided to improve on previous accomplishments by analyzing their data and teacher observation to identify areas of weakness and address them systematically across the grades. Their agreed-upon objective was to create a set of proficiency targets with related instructional strategies and assessment tools in mathematics and language arts for all grade levels. They also agreed to establish consistent mental models such as mind-mapping and concept webbing to assist with linking prior knowledge to new information in order to help students move more easily from the concrete to the abstract. By the end of phase 3 of Project X, teams of teachers had worked together to accomplish their common goal and objectives.

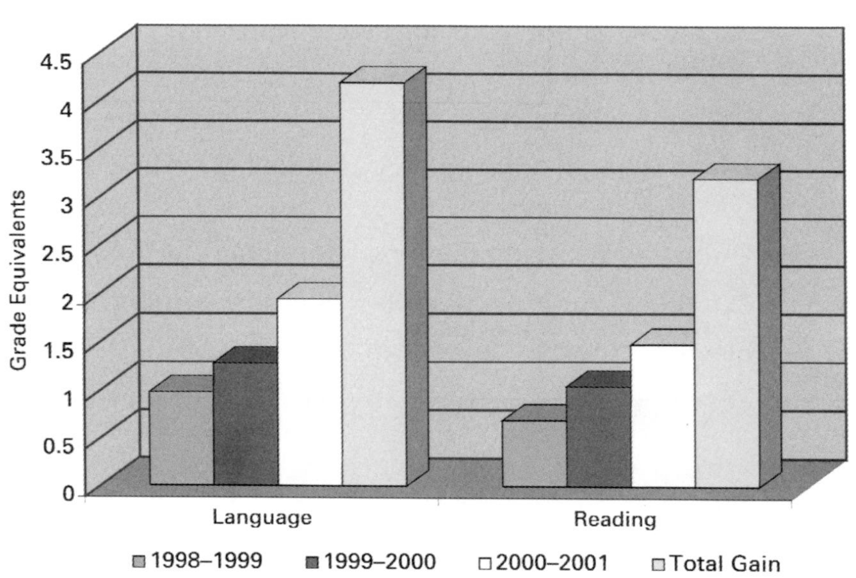

A New Era Begins

In June 2002, Loretta Tetrault retired from her position as principal of Sacred Heart Community School, receiving a fond farewell from the students, staff, and parents who thanked Tetrault for caring so much about them and working so hard with them. In the time that she had been there, the culture of Sacred Heart had been transformed and student achievement levels had improved significantly.

Actions Leading to Success

2002–Ongoing: The Journey Continues

- Brain-activating strategies continue to form the basis for instruction.
- Biweekly staff development sessions continue.
- The baseline testing program continues.
- All teachers work in professional learning communities.
  - Grade-level teams
  - Instructional teams plan integrated units and special themes
- Unique grade combinations continue.
- "Looping" for more seamless learning is initiated.
- Electronic portfolios are explored.

Loretta's successor, Rob Currie, has experienced the effects of reculturing firsthand. He himself has been, in a way, recultured. Coming into Sacred Heart in the wake of Loretta's success, he

understood the need to sustain the momentum that had been built up. With support provided by Loretta and the staff, Rob began the new school year prepared to listen, learn, and lead. Collaborative planning for school and student success continues at Sacred Heart, a Harbor of Hope for all who are there.

Lawrence Heights Middle School: An Ontario Harbor of Hope

As with Sacred Heart Community School, the initial push for school improvement at Lawrence Heights Middle School (LHMS) came from the school principal, Christopher Spence.

The path Chris took to teaching, and eventually to administration, was somewhat circuitous. He played professional football for a while. When an injury forced an early retirement, he spent some time working through the justice system with high-risk youth. He felt, however, that he would have a better chance of helping children and youth if he could work in the schools. He became a teacher and then an administrator. When he was appointed to Lawrence Heights Middle School in Toronto, Chris welcomed the challenge.

"My first love, my first career, was football. When that opportunity no longer existed, education became my football."

—Christopher Spence, Principal,
Lawrence Heights Middle School

Lawrence Heights has a population of approximately 300 students in grades six, seven, and eight, and is situated in a community consisting mostly of public-housing complexes.

Eighty-seven percent of Lawrence Heights' families are immigrants originating from 31 different countries. Twenty-four languages are spoken in the hallways of the school. The crime rate is exceptionally high.

On his first visit to the school, Chris saw defaced bulletin boards, encountered unruly students, and heard of a female teacher being "mooned" by two male students. He also observed students in the library with their feet on tables and saw other students throwing books out of an open window in a contest to see who could throw the farthest. The assembly to introduce him had to be cut short when a fight broke out in the audience.

In his first year at LHMS, Chris spent most of his time dealing with fights, many of which required police intervention. The school that year recorded over 3,000 incidents of students being late for school and a large number of suspensions. Math, reading, and writing scores on standards tests were among the worst in the province. Over half of the staff was discouraged and wanted to transfer to other schools. The situation was desperate.

Building a Culture of Collaboration

Early in his tenure as principal, Chris, like Loretta, realized that he would have to take the lead in bringing change to his school. He also realized that change would be impossible without staff input and commitment. Chris began his work with the staff by sharing his vision for the LHMS learning community—its learners and its staff—along with belief statements and goals for the school. The staff agreed that they would build an environment that would foster learning for all. They committed themselves to the belief that all children can learn, and they agreed that their role as teachers was to help that happen. Their

stated vision required that parents, staff, and the community all be engaged in determining the best strategies for creating an effective learning environment.

Chris introduced the staff to the effective schools research done by Lawrence Lezotte and his associates. They agreed that their top priorities would be to create a safe and orderly environment and a climate of high expectations. Chris knew that the cycle of failure and despair—the lack of hope—that existed at Lawrence Heights would have to be addressed. Many on the staff believed that students at LHMS were both cognitively and linguistically impaired. Chris worked with the staff to study the effects of poverty. They learned that disadvantaged students are seriously at risk in two respects: first, because their behavior patterns, language use, and values do not match those required in typical school settings; and second, because teachers and administrators often do not appropriately assess and address these students' learning needs in order to build on existing strengths. With these new insights in mind, the staff learned to minimize incongruities between school and home by using instructional approaches that incorporated the life experiences and skills of the students. At the same time they worked to help their students understand the school culture, its guidelines, and its boundaries.

"My mission as principal is to bring a vision of dynamic and collaborative leadership to the challenge of public education. The intent of this vision is to build and maintain strong relationships and to encourage commitment and loyalty through trust, growth through participation, and responsibility through accountability. My primary function as the principal is to continually acquire—as well as continually teach those being guided, individually and collectively—the attitudes, beliefs, values, knowledge, and skills that facilitate success and move students and staff to higher levels of performance."

—Christopher Spence, Principal,
Lawrence Heights Middle School

As the Lawrence Heights staff looked for ways to improve their school, the first question was always "How will this benefit our kids?" This question was closely followed by "How will we know it?" The staff began to introduce specific activities that focused on identified needs. We refer to these activities as high-yield strategies and will discuss them in greater detail in chapter 9. Together, Chris and his staff embarked on an exciting journey of school improvement that resulted in the creation of a Harbor of Hope in a school previously characterized by chaos and despair.

Strategies for School and Student Success

Like Sacred Heart, the staff at Lawrence Heights made use of the Correlates of Effective Schools to focus their efforts. In fact, they chose the same two correlates, safe and orderly environment and high expectations for success, as the place to begin their improvement efforts. The staff of Lawrence Heights addressed them with the following strategies.

Safe and Orderly Environment

- A clean and welcoming school
- The good, the bad, and the ugly

- Spectator agreements
- Student involvement
- Silence the violence
- Dress for success

A clean and welcoming school. The staff agreed that they should start with the physical appearance of the building. They knew that a clean, inviting atmosphere would be conducive to beginning the improvement process. Their efforts included the creation of multicultural murals on the walls and lockers. The effect was immediate: the school looked bright, cheerful, and clean.

The good, the bad, and the ugly. Student assemblies focused on student achievement, attendance, attitude, and behavior. Students came to refer to these as "The Good, the Bad, and the Ugly" meetings. Achievements and growth were celebrated, concerns were identified, and goals for improvement were shared. Students were given a "report card" on the climate and culture of Lawrence Heights. Some assemblies were held with the entire student body present, while others were grade-level assemblies.

Spectator agreements. Student spectators at sporting events were viewed as ambassadors for the school whether the event was at home or away. Exemplary behavior was expected and guidelines were spelled out in a written agreement that was signed by all students. Attendance at sporting events was seen as a privilege. Students who did not live up to the spectator agreement lost the privilege for a while.

Student involvement. Class representatives, in collaboration with the staff, held regular meetings in which they developed plans and guidelines for school procedures and special events. The class representatives were responsible for communicating relevant information to their classmates.

The goal of extracurricular activities at LHMS was to promote positive attitudes through building solid relationships and a strong sense of community. Activities like dancing, singing, and drumming created a lot of interest, as did the many opportunities that were provided for students to celebrate their cultural backgrounds.

Silence the violence. Separate stairways were designated for students in grades six and seven in order to minimize bullying and harassment from the older students. Staff maintained a high profile during unstructured times, purposely interacting with high-risk students in an effort to build positive relationships before problems arose.

Dress for success. The Lawrence Heights staff observed that competition among the students about what they wore to school was a problem. When a group of parents proposed that school uniforms be introduced at LHMS, the staff knew that they would have to involve students in the discussion if the idea were to succeed. Students researched the pros and cons of school uniforms, wrote about and debated the subject, and generally explored the issue as it might apply to their school. In the end, both students and parents voted for school uniforms.

Climate of High Expectations for Success

Lawrence Heights addressed this effective schools correlate with the following strategies:

- If you can't measure it, you can't improve it
- Believing in achieving

- Balancing Academics, Sports, and Education (B.A.S.E.)
- Project Pride
- Boys to Men
- Literacy Life and Tech 2000

If you can't measure it, you can't improve it. All LHMS teachers participated in weekly joint planning time with grade-level partners in order to plan for instruction, assessment, and evaluation. Early in the school year, teachers developed a baseline assessment profile of each of their students, with the emphasis placed on reading, writing, mathematics, and social responsibility/character education.

All grade six students at LHMS write the annual provincial assessment in the areas of reading, writing, and mathematics. The staff valued the results of these tests and therefore resolved to develop a parallel assessment for grade eight students in order to track achievement over an extended period.

Believing in achieving. A biweekly reporting process was established to create a sense of urgency around learning. In this way, feedback could be given to individual students on their progress in all subjects as well as in other categories like cooperation, wearing their uniforms, punctuality, and work completion. The progress reports use only "yes" or "no" to indicate if students have shown improvement in each area since the last report, and parent signatures are required. Students who receive a "no" in any category cannot participate in extracurricular activities for the next 2-week period. The message from staff is clear: "If you get a no, you can't go." No exceptions are made. Students rarely receive a "no" more than once. Once the expectations around the progress report were clearly understood, students began to set personal goals of receiving only positive reports in order to receive an "All Yes All Year" shirt at year's end.

Balancing Academics, Sports, and Education (B.A.S.E.). The B.A.S.E. program made participation in sports a reward for academic excellence. In order to participate in sports, students were required to have positive biweekly reports and to present a contract signed by their parent or guardian. They also had to meet academic and behavioral expectations and attend study hall sessions held by the coaches. The message was clear: academic achievement comes first.

Project Pride. Project Pride was introduced to support African-Canadian males in assuming personal responsibility for their own circumstances by challenging them to succeed academically and provide leadership for their families, communities, and school. Students involved in the program received focused support through daily contact with a mentor who also made weekly contact with their parents.

Boys to Men. The Boys to Men program offered after-school activities with caring male role models. The program had strict attendance rules, provided assistance with academics, and focused on pro-social conflict resolution as well as responsible sexual norms.

Literacy Life and Tech 2000. Reluctant readers were given a chance to unlock the power of literacy through the Literacy Life and Tech 2000 program, which had Saturday meetings. Skill-building interventions, book talks, and interactions with guest readers were provided. Technology was used as a tool to support learning.

Celebrating School and Student Success at Lawrence Heights

By June 2000, the provincial test results for grade six students at LHMS rated above both the Toronto and the provincial averages. The incidence of fights had declined to a mere handful and the incidence of tardiness had dropped from 3,000 to less than 400. Lawrence Heights received the Canada Award of Excellence from the National Quality Institute in honor of the organization's commitment to excellence and superior standards. Lawrence Heights Middle School had become a Harbor of Hope.

The school produced a video entitled *Living the Dream* to celebrate its successes and carry the positive message of the school to the community and beyond. Day-by-day improvement and commitment are sometimes difficult to measure. The production of this video helped members of the Lawrence Heights Middle School community look back and recognize the improvements that had been made.

A New Era Begins

In February 2001, Chris Spence was promoted to be superintendent of schools. As he reflected upon his time at Lawrence Heights Middle School, he realized that he had been very fortunate to have had the opportunity to support—and be supported by—a very dedicated staff in the creation of programs and policies to develop a culture of excellence. Chris speaks of becoming an educator because he felt that he had something to offer students. Today, his goal remains unchanged: to provide hope through meeting the needs of students.

Monticello High School: A Harbor of Hope in Virginia

Both Sacred Heart and Lawrence Heights were established schools where the staff, with the leadership of the principal, determined there was a need to improve. The story of Monticello High School (MHS), in Albemarle County, Virginia, is somewhat different.

Monticello opened in 1998 with 914 students from grades 9 through 12 and 95 professional staff. The school was built to relieve overcrowding in the two existing high schools, which were located in very affluent areas. Monticello was built in the district of the county with the lowest socioeconomic profile, where the student body is characterized by high eligibility for subsidized lunch, an unusually high incidence of students with exceptional needs, and a diverse ethnic population. With its opening, catchment areas in the county were revised so that the student body would be drawn from each of the two previously existing high schools as well as from the area immediately surrounding the school. As a new school, Monticello faced challenges before it ever opened.

Irving Jones was the first principal of Monticello High School. Dilemmas for him came early, when many parents from the two existing high schools resisted sending their children to MHS. Monticello was an unknown entity and they feared that the demographics of the new school would translate into an inferior education for their children. When the Virginia Standards of Learning results came in after the first year of the school's operation, their fears seemed justified.

Rather than settle for these results and argue them away on the basis of student background and school location, Irving Jones and the staff viewed the situation as a challenge and an opportunity to chart a fresh course in high school education. They began by taking the bold step of making a public commitment to helping their students reach the state standard in 4 years. With that, they embarked on an ambitious school improvement journey that resulted in their reaching that goal in 2002.

Virginia Standards of Learning (SOL) Pass Rates

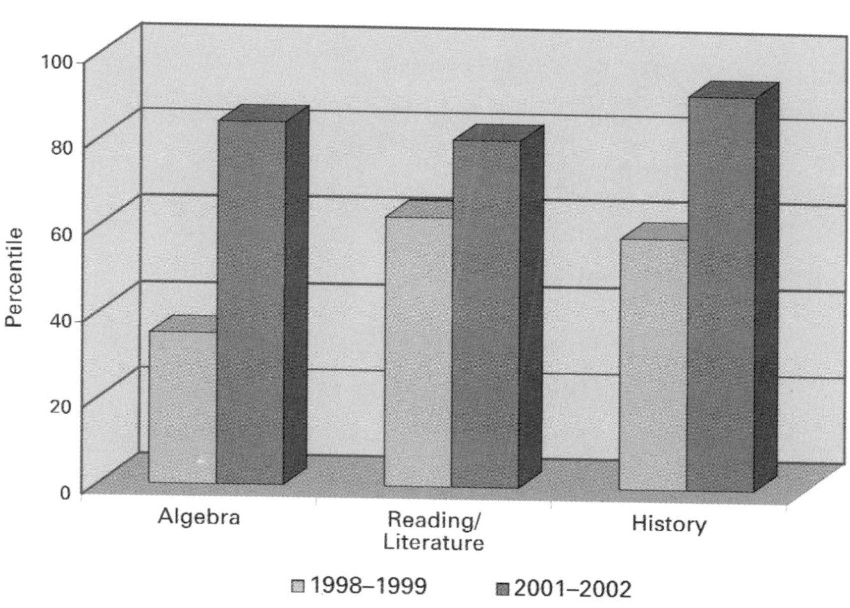

Creating the Culture for School and Student Success

Irving Jones was committed to effective communication among teachers, parents, students, and administrators. Described as a vocal, stubborn, and passionate man, Irving quickly established a hierarchy of importance at Monticello in which students were at the top. One of the first things the staff did was create mission and vision statements to direct their work. Collectively, they articulated the following self-description:

> "We are a community of citizens committed to honor, service, technological competence, and lifelong learning."

Through the creation of their vision statements, the staff of Monticello painted a picture of a high school committed to creating an instructional setting in which students are encouraged to:

- Think critically
- Solve problems creatively
- Find and use resources advantageously
- Communicate effectively

The staff also committed to working in interdisciplinary teams to ensure that:

- Connections were made between instructional content and instructional delivery
- Technology was utilized across and within content areas
- Varied student learning styles and abilities were accommodated
- Instruction was matched to student needs

Identifying the Issues

The staff realized that creating statements of vision and mission did not guarantee that the school would accomplish its goal of academic success for all students. The statements were noble; however, without deliberate planning and action, they would remain just that: statements. The staff knew they would not see

any improvement in student or school success at Monticello without action. With that in mind, they set about gathering critical evidence on student performance in math, reading, and language that would help them understand where to place their professional energy. The information was disaggregated on the basis of gender, ethnicity, free and reduced lunch recipients, and exceptional student needs. The staff discovered that, generally, girls were outperforming boys and that Caucasian students were outperforming most other groups. At the end of three years, the scores had risen dramatically.

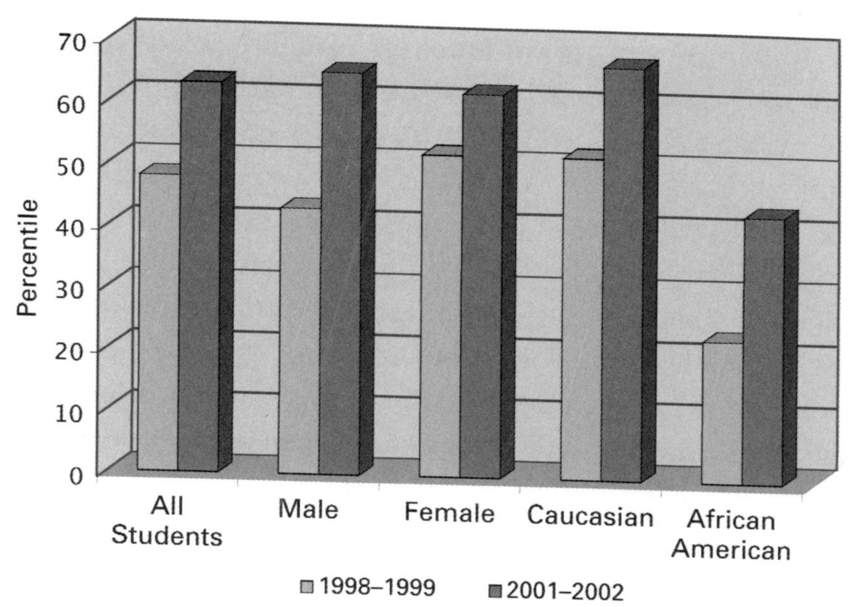

Addressing the Issues

The staff at Monticello translated their statements of vision and mission into action. In so doing, they kept their promise to their community. Using the critical evidence at their disposal, they planned and put into effect the following strategies intended to increase success for all students. Their efforts yielded huge returns. These strategies included:

- Revamped program levels
- Interdisciplinary teaching
- Timetable modification and instructional support
- Mentorship
- Student leadership
- Using data to focus on achievement
- Focusing on the "whole student"

Revamped program levels. Through discussion and by reflecting on student achievement in the various program levels, the staff concluded that motivation was an issue for many students in standard-level courses. They also expressed concern about the challenges of providing this group of students with appropriate instruction and supports. Their solution was to combine standard-level and advanced-level courses to create one course level known as the "academic level." This change increased the expectations for the former standard-level students and allowed staff to focus on instructional strategies to support students in meeting curricular goals in all areas.

Interdisciplinary teaching. Interdisciplinary teaching teams were established to teach the core subject areas of math, science, social studies, and English to same-grade cohorts of students. Joint planning times and common lunch breaks were provided to facilitate the work of teacher teams. Teams collaborated to do vertical curriculum mapping by discipline as well as horizontal

mapping to find commonalities between disciplines. As a result, the staff was able to provide students with a largely integrated instructional setting. They were also able to closely track student progress and, because they were dealing with smaller numbers of students, they were able to intervene early when a student was identified as slipping.

At Monticello, teacher planning rooms are located in different wings of the school, with each one being a "home base" to an interdisciplinary team of eight teachers. This organization of the school removed the physical barriers between departments often found in high schools. Greater proximity between teachers resulted in more contact, both formal and informal. The result was a more coordinated effort to provide optimal instruction and support for all students, including those with exceptional needs.

Through discussion and research, the MHS staff agreed to adopt a resource-based learning approach. Resource-based teaching has reduced teachers' reliance on textbooks and allowed them to make more use of technology and community and learning center resources. This has been a positive step for students, allowing them to pursue their own learning through asking questions and doing the research to find answers.

Timetable modification and instructional support. Time for remedial instruction and mentoring was required to address the needs of all students at Monticello High School. Most of the student body is bussed in, with the result that it is difficult to find time to provide the extra support needed for students who are struggling. A solution was found through the development of a 2-day rotating timetable in which students are taught in seven periods over 2 days. Six of the periods are 90 minutes long and one is 60 minutes long. Ninety-minute periods provide students with more opportunity for in-depth, sustained learning. Every Wednesday, the 60-minute period is used to provide extra time and instruction for those students requiring it.

Mentorship. Mentoring has become a vital function for student support at Monticello and often starts before students even arrive in the school. Grade eight students identified as being potentially high risk upon entry to high school are offered tutoring for 2 weeks during the summer. A Student Leadership Team from MHS teaches them study skills and high school survival techniques.

Teacher mentorship is also a critical feature of student support at Monticello. All grade nine students are placed in groups of 12 to 15, and each group is assigned to a teacher who will mentor and guide them during their 4 years at Monticello. The teacher mentor is someone who does not have them in any of his or her courses.

The groups meet once a month for about an hour to discuss student-generated topics such as bullying, impaired driving, and other related issues. The teacher mentors also assist students with course selection, career exploration, relationship problems, and a myriad of other things. The fact that these are multi-age groups presents a natural opportunity for older students to mentor younger students as well.

Student leadership. The greatest resources in a school are the students. Student mentors help struggling peers with academic work. Conflict-resolution teams are trained to assist with problem-solving and conflict management. A Reserve Officers'

Training Corps (ROTC) program also provides leadership opportunities to students.

With the assistance of the Annenberg Foundation, service learning has been introduced into the 12th-grade program. Students participating in service learning research community needs and use their findings to plan and implement programs responsive to the needs of local nonprofit organizations. The students also create strategies for assessing the effectiveness of the programs they have devised. Through service learning, students have researched and completed projects pertaining to such things as protecting the environment, beautifying the community, and supporting the local animal shelter.

Using data to focus on achievement. Early in the life of the school, Irving Jones and the staff at Monticello established what they call the Achievement Team to facilitate communication and support between the school and the central office. The work of the team is closely tied to the Monticello school improvement plan. It consists of the district coordinators of technology, math, science, English, and social studies as well as school curriculum leaders, and it meets monthly to review assessment results as well as plan for enrichment, intervention, and review. The team also plans and facilitates professional development. This interdisciplinary connection between school and the district office has assisted with the work to eliminate the performance gap between African-American and Caucasian students. It has also had significant positive impact on the state Standards of Learning scores for Monticello.

Since schools in Virginia and other parts of the United States are measured on their Standards of Learning (SOL) test scores in English, math, history, and science, it is important to the staff that they reach the accreditation level. To that end, time is spent preparing students to take the tests. Those students who do not do well on the SOL tests receive intensive support to prepare them to retake the test. During the 2002–2003 school year, 275 of the 1,094 students at MHS were involved in this kind of support.

The staff of MHS does not measure the school's success only by the state Standards of Learning scores. A variety of classroom-based assessments are used, as well as End of Course assessments (EOCs), to track achievement. Data obtained in this way provide evidence for teachers on the impact of their instruction and also provide information for planning future instruction. Additional student performance indicators include such things as graduation rates; post-graduation plans; the type of diploma earned (advanced, standard, IEP); number of students in Advanced Placement, Honors, and Advanced courses; and the number of students in standard and practical level courses.

As the staff at MHS found increased uses for data to inform their structures and instruction, they identified a need for help with its collection and interpretation. As a result, a half-time position has been created for a school testing coordinator. This person coordinates the writing of the Standards of Learning tests and is also responsible for training teachers to administer them, tracking the writing to ensure that no students are missed, communicating with the state's department of education, and organizing test data in ways that allow the staff to use the results in support of student success and achievement.

Focusing on the "whole student." Although Monticello High School has a strong focus on academic success, there is an equally strong focus on the "whole student." The staff recognizes

that a positive self-image supports student achievement in all areas. For that reason, they strive to offer a variety of programs that will foster the mental, emotional, and physical well-being of all students.

Each Wednesday, the timetable has been arranged to provide an hour for co-curricular activities during the school day. To compensate for the fact that most students are bussed to school, late busses are run to allow students to be part of school life beyond the classroom at Monticello High School.

A New Era Begins

In 2003, Irving Jones was named the MetLife/NASSP National High School Principal of the Year. He has since become a senior administrator for the Richmond, Virginia, public schools. Over the course of his 5 years at Monticello, Irving made an indelible mark on the community. The student population has risen to 1,066 and in January 2002 the school met its publicly stated commitment to achieve full accreditation. Monticello High School has won the respect and confidence of its community.

During his time at MHS, Irving developed a staff that became stable and productive. Staff members say it is not hard to stay on the path that was created because they were always involved in the planning and policymaking. In the words of staff member Diane Clark, "He led so everybody thought they were doing it themselves. Jones had a vision, and he knew how to collect on it" (*Principal Leadership,* January, 2003, p. 44).

In September 2003, the new principal, Billy Haun, moved to Monticello from one of its feeder schools. He is grateful for the strong foundation that he has inherited, and he is committed to supporting the initiatives already in place at MHS. In addition, he has identified a need for the coordination of programs and services for students with exceptional learning needs. He would also like to see more students earning college credits as part of their high school experience. Monticello High School is a Harbor of Hope for all who are there.

The three Harbors of Hope schools we have described serve different communities and different age groups. They are examples of how a culture of optimism and hope is created when students, staff, and parents work together to focus on improved learning outcomes. While each of these schools used unique structures and processes to accomplish their goals, they have many characteristics in common. Chapter 2 provides an overview of what we have learned about the mindsets and actions that are needed when schools commit to offering hope and success for all students.

Chapter 2

Harbors of Hope: What We Have Learned

Stephen Covey (1989) makes the point that highly effective people have strong character combined with high levels of competence. We believe that schools that are effective also have strong character combined with high levels of competence. People and schools with character are principle-centered. They value qualities such as fairness, integrity, and honesty. Human dignity and the principles of potential, growth, and patience underpin all interactions with students, staff, or parents. "Principles are not practices," writes Covey. "They are deep, fundamental truths that have universal application" (p. 35). When principles become part of a school's culture, they provide a foundation for the development of practices that will nurture and encourage all members of the school community.

Principle-centered educators are passionate about what they do. Michael Fullan (2001a) identifies moral purpose as essential to changing school cultures, explaining that "it is about both ends and means. In education, an important end is to make a difference in the lives of students. But the means of getting to that end are also crucial" (p. 13). In other words, when individuals care enough to do good work, they develop the competencies necessary for success. They learn about the change process, develop relationship skills, create and share the knowledge that will make a difference in student achievement, and commit to aligned practices.

The three schools featured in chapter 1 all recognized a need to offer more for their students. This provided incentive for staff to come together to create principle-centered communities of caring around their students and to develop the competencies that would lead to success for all students.

Hope Is the Underlying Principle

As is the case with schools everywhere, the three schools we identified as Harbors of Hope have groups of students who struggle with achievement. Students who do not experience school success live with low achievement and with the discouragement and hopelessness that can come with it. They find themselves on a continuum that spirals downward, beginning with a state of anxiety over being unable to achieve school success, and moving through feelings of helplessness as they head for complete loss of hope.

The children who struggle in school are also the ones who often either cause the most disruption or are the most "invisible." Either way, these children are seriously at risk. Daniel Goleman (1998), in his work on emotional intelligence, points out that failure in school has a significant negative impact on the development of emotional intelligence. When the development of emotional intelligence is delayed, the result is usually poor attendance, behavior, and attitudes. The end result is low achievement.

Fortunately, as Goleman points out, a person's level of emotional intelligence is not genetically fixed, nor does it develop only in childhood. In fact, it continues to develop as one learns from life experiences. Emotional intelligence can be developed and continue growing, regardless of age.

The staff in the three schools we have written about believed that if they could find ways to offer their students hope, they would begin to see improvement in achievement and, with that, increased emotional intelligence and feelings of competence. They also realized that simply being hopeful was not enough. Action was required if they were to successfully support their students and impart the hope they were committed to providing.

Michael Fullan (1997) defines hope as the capacity to not panic in tight situations but rather to find ways and resources to deal with difficult issues. He dispels the notion that hope is a naïve view of the world—the blind hopefulness attributed to those who cannot bear to look at the realities of life. Fullan links hope with purpose, not naïveté. He groups wishful thinking, blind hopefulness, and cynicism together, separating them from hope. Fullan holds that hopeful people are very aware of reality and that it is their hopefulness that allows them to remain optimistic in spite of what may appear to be insurmountable odds.

Hope without action is little more than wishful thinking. Thomas Sergiovanni (2004) speaks of hope and faith as going together, with faith coming from "commitment to a cause and a strong belief in a set of ideas" (p. 34). He draws a compelling distinction between wishful leaders and hopeful leaders. Although he speaks specifically of those in formal leadership positions, we contend that teachers should be included here because they are leaders in learning. The chart on page 42 provides valuable guidance to those concerned with student and school success when the focus is hope.

A Wishful Stance	A Hopeful Stance
Passive Reaction	*Active Reaction*
• "I wish these kids would behave."	• "I hope these kids behave. What can I do to help?"
• No faith to back up their wishes	• Faith in assumptions and ideas
• No pathways to action	• Pathways to action
• No action	• Action
• No change	• Change

Each of the three schools in chapter 1 adopted the hopeful stance. They combined the character of holding hope with the competencies of acquiring and applying those strategies that would lead to success. As a result, they became Harbors of Hope.

The Influence of Effective Schools Research

Effective schools research led the way into the exploration of school improvement more than 35 years ago, and it is as relevant today as it was then. We worried that some readers might discount the work spoken of here as being attached to the past and therefore not applicable in today's schools. The fact is that correlates of effective schools and effective school research have lasted, while other educational planning concepts have disappeared. We believe this is because the correlates are based on

empirical observation of school outcomes. Many writers in the area of school improvement focus on input, believing that the introduction of the "right" program or of specific teacher training will improve schools. Effective schools research, on the other hand, has always focused on measurable outcomes. Improving schools have specific common characteristics—the correlates of effective schools. None of the correlates stands alone. In fact, when a school demonstrates improvement, all of the correlates are present and interconnected to create the culture and climate that result in student and school success.

The Seven Correlates of Effective Schools

1. Instructional leadership
2. Clear and focused mission
3. Safe and orderly environment
4. Climate of high expectations for success
5. Frequent monitoring of student progress
6. Positive home-school relations
7. Opportunity to learn and time on task

When one reads the current literature on school improvement, the influence of effective schools research and the correlates is evident. Richard DuFour and Robert Eaker (1998) reference Lezotte and the correlates of effective schools in *Professional Learning Communities at Work*. Robert Marzano (2003), in *What Works in Schools*, identifies 11 factors affecting student achievement. We believe the factors he identifies as school- or teacher-based are extensions of the effective school correlates. This is confirmed in his summary: "Thirty-five years of research provides remarkably clear guidance as to the steps schools can take to be highly effective in enhancing student achievement" (p. 11).

Today, in the Parkland School District near Edmonton, Alberta, the school improvement process is being driven through the correlates of effective schools. Also in Alberta, the High Prairie School District is basing all of its school improvement work on the effective schools research. The school-based administrator evaluation process uses the correlates as its foundation in the Ontario school district of Rainy River. The Catholic School Board in Regina, Saskatchewan, also uses the correlates to support its school improvement initiatives. Even reports to the Board of Trustees reference the correlate that will be addressed as a result of any action they are considering. While we have specifically highlighted the work done at Sacred Heart Community School, the fact is that every school in the Regina Catholic School District uses the correlates to support improvement initiatives. The district is aligned. The elected officials, the senior administration, school administrators, and teachers all understand the correlates and effective schools research.

In the United States, many districts are basing their school improvement work on the Correlates of Effective Schools. Hays Consolidated Independent School District in Kyle, Texas, for example, is using surveys effectively to obtain critical evidence on its performance on the correlates. The survey results then form the basis for the district's school improvement plans. The Superintendency Institute of America has been meeting for the past 13 years to explore effective schools research and the correlates. It is led by Ruth and Lawrence Lezotte and is an organization

of over 120 superintendents of education who meet twice a year to share new research and strategies for improving schools and meeting the mission of learning for all.

The influence of effective schools research is long standing and wide spread. Throughout Canada and the United States, schools and school districts are using it, along with the correlates, in their improvement efforts. The districts and organizations mentioned above are just a few of them. As schools and districts improve, knowledge about what constitutes an effective school and the interdependence between the correlates continues to grow.

Applying the Correlates in Harbors of Hope

Correlates are the characteristics that are consistently present in schools that are positively impacting student achievement, behavior, attitude, and attendance. The three schools we have described as Harbors of Hope used the correlates and effective schools research as the basis for their improvement efforts.

Instructional leadership. All three schools presented in chapter 1 had the benefit of effective instructional leaders. All of the principals had visions of what would make their schools better places, and they were committed to the concept of continuous improvement through research, planning, and evaluation. They were passionate in their belief that all children can achieve and that it is the mandate of schools to ensure "Learning for All—Whatever It Takes" (Lezotte and McKee, 2002). They all understood that the prime purpose of school is to ensure that all students learn, and they made it their goal to be knowledgeable about current practice in curriculum, instruction, and assessment. In all cases, the administrators were vigilant, insisting that the stated values, vision, and purpose be reflected in all interactions between students, staff, and the parent community. They had moral purpose and were willing to challenge the status quo.

As formal leaders in their schools, the principals of Sacred Heart, Lawrence Heights, and Monticello recognized that a sense of order and discipline was imperative so that teachers could focus on instruction. They were persistent and energetic, highly visible in their schools. Committed to building on the talents of their staff members, these leaders empowered their staffs to participate fully in the development of school improvement plans, and they provided the resources necessary for plans to be implemented. These principals knew that leadership, both formal and informal, must be shared among staff, students, and parents. They knew that the impact of informal leadership in a school would be only as strong as the support it received from the formal leaders. As a result, they encouraged those people on their staff who demonstrated initiative and exhibited leadership qualities. As staff developed plans to achieve goals, the principals supported, affirmed, and facilitated those efforts. As goals were met, they cheered and celebrated. Teamwork and collaboration were highly valued and, in fact, expected. Learning was the driving force and all of the initiatives that were introduced focused on the impact they would have on learning.

Clear and focused mission. In all three schools staff members created a compelling vision and a focused statement of mission that provided direction and influenced all decision making. As their work evolved, catch phrases developed that seemed to capture their stated vision and mission. Monticello's "Kids come first" and "To teach them you have to reach them" are simple, focused statements of what that school values. At

Sacred Heart, the staff committed to the creation of a "no violence sanctuary" and to high expectations for all within a family atmosphere. At Lawrence Heights, "Believing in Achieving" became the summary phrase. In all cases, the mission of the schools was to improve learning for all students.

Safe and orderly environment. All three schools made a safe and orderly environment a priority because when students feel safe they are more able to take the risks necessary to learn. All schools developed guidelines to communicate boundaries and expectations for students. At the same time, the staff in each school worked conscientiously to build strong relationships with the students, each other, and parents. At Sacred Heart, the Responsibility Plan provides guidance for students and staff about expected behaviors. Discipline at Sacred Heart is viewed as an opportunity to nurture and teach. The Lawrence Heights staff believes strongly that their adoption of a standard school uniform for all students has greatly alleviated stress and problems among students. Staff at all three schools actively support students by being present and visible during unstructured times. In all cases, school assemblies reinforce expectations for behavior and celebrate successes.

All of the schools realized the importance of the physical appearance of the school. One of the first actions taken at Lawrence Heights was to create a "clean and welcoming school," a place of pride for everyone. At Sacred Heart the "family atmosphere" to which they were committed has been created using colorful posters and learning props along with comfortable furniture and plants. The Monticello staff started with a new building and has worked diligently to keep it in good condition, free from graffiti and vandalism.

Climate of high expectations for success. Creating a climate of high expectations for success was also a priority in each school. Staff members focused their energies on finding the structures and strategies that would enable their students to succeed. Sacred Heart became a "brain activating oasis," with teachers using what they knew about brain-based learning, multiple intelligences, learning styles, and differentiated instruction. The Lawrence Heights staff adopted the "Believing in Achieving" motto and committed to biweekly progress reports that provided the basis for the "if you get a no, you can't go" rule. They also developed structures like the B.A.S.E. (Balancing Academics, Sports, and Education), Project Pride, Boys to Men, and Literacy Life and Tech 2000 to support academic achievement. At Monticello High School, the staff studied the Standards of Learning results and later expanded their focus to include formative assessments and end-of-course evaluations as guides to instructional practice. The staff there is so committed to using data to inform their instruction and improvement efforts that they have used a portion of their staff allocation to hire a testing coordinator to assist them in their efforts. Monticello students at all points on the achievement continuum are identified and involved in programming to support their growth and achievement.

Frequent monitoring of student progress. Critical evidence was used to monitor achievement and measure student growth in all three schools. Teachers were provided with time for team planning based on what the data and critical evidence were telling them. Teacher teams articulated essential learning outcomes in core subject areas and planned instruction to reach their stated outcomes. All schools focused on improving provincial or state assessment scores, and all used school- and classroom-based

tools for both formative and summative assessments to inform their instruction.

Positive home-school relations. The importance of involving parents as partners in their children's education was recognized in all schools. Personal contacts and regular reporting functions were in place in all of the schools. All of the schools encountered some challenges in their attempt to involve parents; however, none let this deter their efforts. They realized that parents want their children to succeed and that they will be supportive if they believe the school cares about their children's success. Staff at all schools made concerted efforts to build solid home-school relationships.

Opportunity to learn and time on task. All of the schools found ways to maximize opportunities for students to learn. Individual student achievement was monitored and, where necessary, extra time and support for learning were provided. At Monticello the timetable was modified to allow for teacher and student mentoring as well as for intervention where students were struggling. At Sacred Heart, an altered school day and alternative plans for recess and lunch reduced unstructured times that were disrupting instructional time. They completely revamped their Learning Resource program in order to provide more direct support to students. In addition, they implemented structures such as student mentors and "hallway huddles" to support learning. Lawrence Heights established the B.A.S.E. program along with the Life Literacy and Tech 2000 program so that students could be supported through tutoring. Their "Believing in Achieving" biweekly progress reports stressed attendance, punctuality, and homework completion as well as continuous improvement in all subject areas.

Harbors of Hope Do Not Just Happen

All schools plan, but many do not plan to improve. Sometimes schools may focus on implementing a new program, process, or activity and believe that they have planned to improve. But initiatives are only as good as the results they produce. Schools must ask, "Do the new initiatives result in improved student achievement?" If the answer to that question is not yes, the school has not really planned to improve. To ascertain whether new programs, processes, or activities are, in fact, resulting in improvement, schools must find ways to measure growth over time. Effective school improvement initiatives are focused on doing what is required to enhance student achievement.

In his work with schools throughout Canada and the United States, Wayne Hulley has encountered many different approaches to school planning. The three schools we call Harbors of Hope all planned to improve school and student success. In the process, they used data to ensure that the programs they implemented had a positive impact on learning. This shift from planning to implement to planning to improve learning is the secret to creating a Harbor of Hope. Hulley believes that some schools are more effective than others and that the school a student attends matters. As a result of his work, he has identified the following principles that are consistently used by effective schools as they plan.

- Plan success for all students.
- Focus on improving student achievement.
- Realize that improved student behavior, attendance, and attitudes will impact achievement.
- Be guided by a shared purpose, clearly stated.

- Use measures of student achievement and other critical evidence in planning for improvement as well as for monitoring and adjusting the plan as needed to achieve goals.
- Establish professional learning communities in which staff can collaborate.
- Plan to improve and then monitor progress toward goals.
- Use time and staff to enhance learning outcomes.
- Set clear goals to direct action and evaluate progress.
- Implement high-yield strategies to reach goals.

Alignment Is the Foundation for Successful School Improvement

There are multiple levels of influence in education: classroom, school, district, provincial/state, and national. When school priorities for improvement are aligned with district and provincial or state priorities, time and resources can be devoted to facilitating planning for student and school success. This kind of alignment benefits classroom teachers and, ultimately, students.

Experience has shown us that individual schools improve more rapidly and more profoundly when the Planning for School and Student Success Process is also a stated goal of the district. Senior administrators and elected officials have a major role to play. Michael Fullan (Fullan, Bertani, & Quinn, 2004) points out that in addition to understanding pedagogy and the change process, effective district leaders:

> . . . know how to use the key advantages that their positions afford them for implementing their vision: they have the mandate from the board that appointed them, the big picture of the organization because of their position in it, a

Alignment for School and Student Success

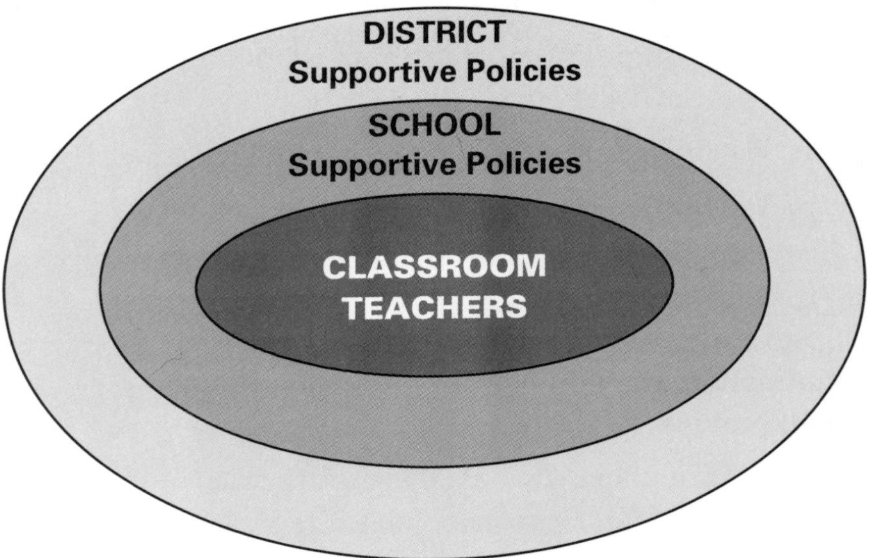

public forum and visibility, and control over the financial and human resources necessary for bringing about change. (p. 43)

Fullan, Bertani, and Quinn maintain that effective district leaders have a "driving conceptualization" of what constitutes successful district improvement. They say that "high engagement with others in the district and plenty of two-way communication that deepens shared ownership and commitment" are required to implement a leader's vision. Effective district administrators have much the same impact on district-wide improvement as principals do on improvement in their schools.

In Saskatchewan, Gwen Keith, the director of Regina Catholic Schools, was able to work with school board members and the Department of Education to modify the school day for Sacred

Heart Community School in order to support the work the teachers believed needed to be done. The unique combined classes they conceived of, also with her support, have proven to be an integral part of the Sacred Heart culture. The superintendent of the district in which Monticello High School is located is Kevin Castner. He stated in his address to staff for the 2003–2004 school year that "instruction can't just be successful for some students; it must be successful for all. We have to engage the hearts and minds of all children so they can do quality work that will help them become successful adults. That's the business of education." The Toronto District School Board fully supported the innovative programs that were introduced at Lawrence Heights.

The High Prairie School District in Alberta is certainly demonstrating the power of district-wide and provincial leadership for school and student success. Supported by Alberta Learning, the High Prairie School District is in the second phase of funding for school improvement. Called the Alberta Initiative for School Improvement (AISI), the mandate of this initiative is to support and facilitate school improvement efforts through professional development and the provision of needed structures and resources. As part of their plan, during the 2003–2004 school year every school in the High Prairie School District created a school success team which worked with Wayne Hulley over a period of 7 months. During their work together, the teams were given the background and the materials to begin planning for the school and student success processes at their schools. The teams had the opportunity to begin working at their schools within a context of collaboration and professional support that allowed them to learn together over an extended period of time. Significant strides were made during the year using this training method.

This work has been supported and extended during the 2004–2005 school year. In October, Linda Dier facilitated a 2-day seminar for school and central office administrators on their role in supporting school improvement initiatives. Wayne Hulley built on that work in November when he undertook a school-by-school "quest" in which he asked focused questions to determine levels of commitment and actions taken regarding the school improvement plans that had been established. These activities are part of the sustainability plan for the district.

Professional Learning Communities Are the Forum for Collaboration

The work of Rick DuFour and Bob Eaker (1998) on the power of collaboration through the development of professional learning communities (PLCs) has had a significant impact on schools and school improvement. We will focus more deeply on the work of PLCs later in the book; however, at this point it is important to note that we perceive of professional learning communities functioning in different configurations at many levels within a school district.

At the district level, decisions made and processes developed have an enormous impact on students and schools; therefore, it is important that all district-level staff work as a PLC to collaborate in order to focus their support for learning and improved outcomes. At the school level, staff members function interdependently as a PLC to plan for structures and processes that will benefit all students in their school. Within this view of the PLC, the school staff works collectively on school-wide goals. In addition, teachers also work in more focused PLC team settings to collaborate on specific goals established for specific groups of students.

An aligned school district is one that realizes that learning is the business they are in and that structures, systems, and processes must be developed to support student success. In this organization, everyone in the district sees him- or herself as a member of a professional learning community committed to supporting achievement. As a result, we have a number of PLCs, each with a different focus, but all committed to student learning. Teachers function as members of the district PLC which offers professional and financial support. They are also members of the whole-school PLC which asks, "How will we work together for the benefit of all students in our school?" Finally, they are members of smaller professional learning community teams that develop very specific goals and actions to meet the needs of the students with whom they work daily.

As we develop our concept of planning for school and student success, we will often refer to professional learning communities in the plural. This is to recognize the fact that professionals must work together at all levels and in a variety of ways in order to meet the needs of all students.

Summary

Harbors of Hope are wonderful places. Data collected through surveys and interviews indicate that as student achievement improves, all of the staff, students, and parents in the school community become more positive. Students feel more attached to their teachers and the school. Teachers express greater professional satisfaction, and parents show an increased level of support for schools and for education in general. Effective schools research has shown that increased levels of achievement will positively affect student behavior, attendance, and attitudes. When schools focus on success for all students, a positive culture is created that can be observed beyond the classroom—on playgrounds, in hallways, and even in staff lounges.

Altering a school culture to create a Harbor of Hope is not easy. The prospect of changing timetables, modifying assessment strategies, introducing professional learning communities, teaching for success, using critical evidence to guide planning, and taking responsibility for results obtained may cause many staff members to resist. People seldom embrace change without first feeling nervous and insecure. What we have observed in schools that are on the school improvement journey, though, is that when results of change initiatives are successful, satisfaction increases and a momentum builds that makes "Learning for All—Whatever It Takes" a reality.

The chapters that follow provide a proven path to creating Harbors of Hope and more successful schools.

Chapter 3

Harbors of Hope: A Proven Approach

We have spoken of the importance of reculturing in a school if it is to become a Harbor of Hope. We encourage schools to *plan to improve* and to move beyond wishful thinking to an attitude of purposeful hope. How does a school plan to improve, and then actually improve? What kinds of changes are necessary? The key activity is collaboration. The key concept is hope. And the key approach is what we call the Planning for School and Student Success Process.

The Planning for School and Student Success Process was developed by Wayne Hulley after a review of the educational research and as a result of his work with schools across North America. It is a cyclical, self-perpetuating model for continuous improvement that is closely aligned with the Effective School Process developed by Lawrence Lezotte. It is based on a simple concept of change, the See-Do-Get cycle, that has been used by many writers and researchers to explain the way things are currently and what it takes to make meaningful change.

The See-Do-Get cycle explains that individuals or organizations get the results they deserve as a result of the things they are doing. What they are doing is based on their belief systems, habits, and culture; therefore, meaningful change results first from seeing things in a new way and then from taking different actions that will lead to different and hopefully improved results. The culture will change.

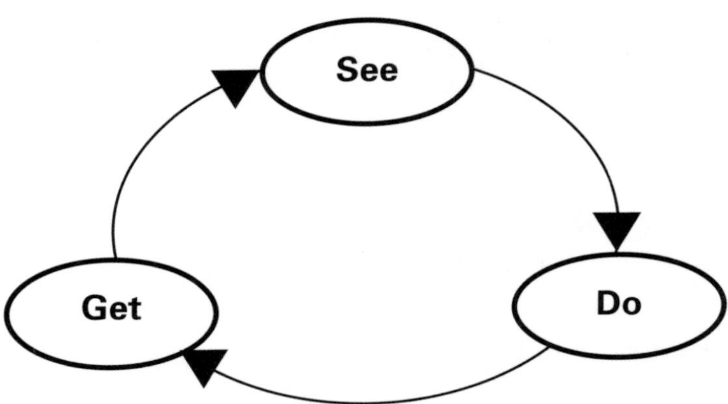

We would like to add a word at this point about the power of a hopeful stance in the See-Do-Get cycle. With hope and its accompanying optimism, the results of actions taken will be viewed in a positive light. If goals are met, those who met them have good reason to be satisfied. If, however, goals are not met, those who tried to meet the goals can still learn a lot from the process and apply what they learn to future action. The teaching and learning process is complex and often ambiguous. Hope fueled by optimism and passion will keep educators engaged in a continuous improvement process.

The importance of reculturing, of comprehensive, organic change, must be emphasized. As Michael Fullan (1997) points

out, linear planning has never changed a school: "current strategies—top-down, bottom-up or sideways—don't work. We need to step back from this conundrum and approach it differently, more basically and as usual in postmodern times, more paradoxically" (p. 219). According to Fullan:

> The situation of change is profoundly problematic and we are down to our last virtue: hope. We stand less of a chance by pursuing the techniques of innovation than we do by working on a deeper understanding of the complex interrelationships of emotions, hope, empathy and moral purpose. (p. 221)

The Planning for School and Student Success Process (PSSSP) shown on page 60 stresses the importance of focused study and reflection in determining the current level of student achievement and how the school is viewed by students, staff, and parents. Test scores are considered, of course, but also important is feedback from students, staff, and parents. Such information is essential during the goal-setting stage if the process is to have a positive impact on student achievement and on school culture in general. It provides a vehicle for professional reflection, conversation, planning, and support that will allow a school staff to work together to make a difference for students.

You may wonder why we refer to this approach as the Planning for School and Student Success Process rather than the Planning for Student and School Success Process. Subsequent chapters in this book will focus on the importance of shared leadership, professional learning communities, curriculum alignment, and flexible structures in improving the learning outcomes for all students. We believe that the strength of a school is in its staff and that staff members can exert a more significant influence on student learning by working together than by working alone. When teachers work together and begin to see themselves as responsible for all students in the school, the result is a greater capacity to deal effectively with the broad array of demands that they face. For this reason, we place "school" first in our title. When the school as a whole is effective, all students will reap the benefits. The synergy and interdependence that result from strong collaborative relationships can only lead to improved learning. Thus, placing the school first in the planning process has the paradoxical effect of placing students first overall.

The Planning for School and Student Success Process

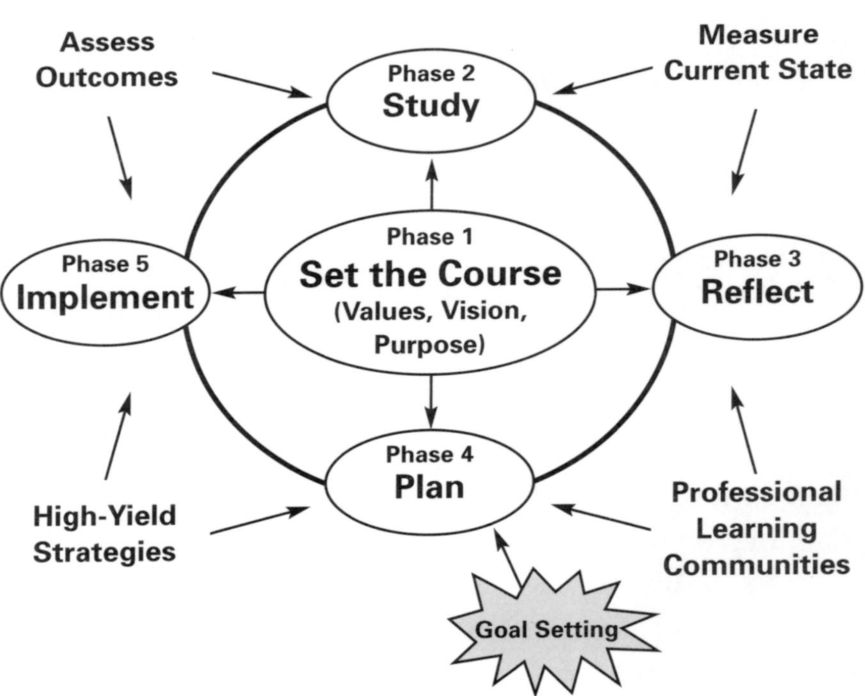

This diagram of the Planning for School and Student Success Process shows the relationship of the five phases in the process: set the course, study, reflect, plan, and implement.

Phase 1—Set the Course (Values, Vision, Purpose)

The first phase involves the entire staff in the creation of a statement of shared values, vision, and purpose. Values determine behaviors. Having a discussion on values engages the hearts of those who participate. Through these discussions, the staff identifies what is important to them and clarifies their beliefs about school life and the work of teaching and learning. When a staff identifies their shared value of learning, the next step is to ask, "Are all students learning?"

If the staff does not begin with a discussion on values and instead begins by gathering and analyzing data, the process becomes head-driven. This will lead to a tendency to rationalize and assign blame: "No wonder the scores are low: look at the homes they come from! No wonder the scores are low: they never do their homework. No wonder the scores are low: they couldn't read or do math when I got them. Don't they teach anything at the lower grade levels?" And on it goes. The reflection and sharing that are embedded in the process of identifying values are extremely important. It is not possible to articulate one's personal values without becoming emotionally involved. The collective identification of staff values provides a foundation for their work together.

Vision statements offer a picture of the future the staff wants to create for the students, themselves, and the school. Staff members need to ask themselves: "How will the values we have identified be evident in the kind of school community we will create?" The answers to this question will help the staff create a vision statement.

The purpose statement is a simple statement intended to inspire those who read it and to provide guidance for all decisions made and actions taken. A statement such as "our purpose is to create hope and success for all" is intended to inspire and direct staff as they tackle their fundamental mandate, which is "Learning for All—Whatever It Takes."

Phase 2—Study

In the study phase, the focus is on gathering data or critical evidence in the areas that are important for future planning. It is important in this phase to "measure what matters." There is an overabundance of data in schools, and only some of it will be relevant for school improvement. We refer to the most relevant data as "critical evidence."

Once staff have clearly identified and stated their values, they will be in a position to gather and organize related critical evidence. The staff can formulate questions about the current success of their school and students and then gather critical evidence that will help them answer those questions. Once the critical evidence is available, goals can be set and planning can begin. If the staff has declared that learning is something they value, then critical evidence about student achievement will be important to them.

This is a refreshing approach for schools that have been required, in the past, to focus on data that others have identified as important. Our experience has been that when educators have a voice in the process and in identifying the assistance they require, they will willingly study and use data to improve

achievement. If, however, they are told what they should care about and are expected to use data to create a report for someone else, their commitment and support for the process will be seriously undermined.

Phase 3—Reflect

The reflection phase is closely related to the study phase. Reflection involves organizing the critical evidence in ways that are meaningful to the staff. It is at this point in the Planning for School and Student Success Process that professional learning communities (PLCs) are created to focus on responding to what the data are telling them. When staff members are organized into professional learning communities, they can reflect more deeply on the information that has been gathered. Working collaboratively, they can evaluate the critical evidence to determine what it is telling them about the achievement of students they teach. This process forms the foundation for subsequent planning and results in more meaningful goal setting. The professional learning community concept is discussed in more detail in chapter 8.

Phase 4—Plan

In the planning phase, critical evidence gathered previously is used to set goals. When it comes to goal setting, educators can typically find a myriad of things they feel they could be doing better. As a result, they sometimes set too many goals at once. The inevitable end result is discouragement when considerable time and effort have been expended with minimal results. In the PSSSP, we recommend that each PLC establish no more than three goals on which to focus their energy. The only stipulation is that the goals lead to improved learning.

We recommend that educators use the SMART goals strategy when planning for school and student success. Conzemius and O'Neill (2002) tell us that SMART goals are **S**trategic and specific, **M**easurable, **A**ttainable, **R**esults-based, and **T**ime-bound. Used effectively, SMART goals help a staff focus and enhance the planning process because such goals focus on demonstrable outcomes that can be realized within a reasonable timeframe.

Professional learning communities can select a variety of approaches, structures, and practices to help them reach their goals. Implementation plans involve looking at the research and case literature to determine strategies that have the greatest potential of ensuring that the goals are met. We call these "high-yield strategies."

The goals and implementation plans of each of the professional learning communities form the basis for the school's improvement plan.

Phase 5—Implement

The implementation phase involves beginning to use the high-yield strategies that have been chosen to meet the goals that have been set. It is important that PLCs have the time and support they need to meet regularly. Their job is to plan, implement, support, and monitor. The monitoring function of this phase involves collecting critical evidence on the impact of the new approaches being implemented. This information then forms the basis for a return to the study phase, where the cycle for continuous improvement begins once more.

The Planning for School and Student Success Process is truly a cyclical, self-perpetuating model for continuous improvement and growth.

Summary

The Planning for School and Student Success Process offers a pathway to school success. This model has been used in numerous school districts across North America and has been proven to support the effective schools mission of "Learning for All—Whatever It Takes." It is not offered as a fill-in-the-blanks approach to school improvement; instead, it is offered as a planning template designed to facilitate an authentic improvement process.

We believe schools should keep two important questions in mind as they work:

1. Are we planning to improve? (as opposed to planning to plan or planning to implement new activities)
2. Are we collectively committed to doing what is required to provide support so *all* students can be successful?

It is our belief—and our experience—that the Planning for School and Student Success Process provides a structure for purposeful change in classrooms and schools that will result in a culture of hope. Structure, however, does not guarantee positive change. Schools change and improve as a result of staff action. In part 2, we look at actions and strategies that can change schools and influence student success.

Part 2

Strategies for Creating Harbors of Hope

Chapter 4

Plan to Improve: Who Is in Charge?

During the 1980s and early 1990s, the common view in effective schools research was that the principal was the key to shaping school culture and effecting reform. The literature from that period reflects an assumption that a school's principal, by holding high expectations and directing teachers' activities, would cause teachers to work cooperatively and would thus create an effective school. In other words, the principal was the shop foreman ensuring that workers were toeing the line.

Early improvement efforts tended to focus on structural rather than cultural issues. Attention was given to things like altering schedules, revising class composition, and implementing new programs. The movement to site-based planning during those years was an attempt to give schools the authority for local decision-making. None of these strategies had the desired impact because nothing was done to alter the culture at either the school or district level.

Current research has shown that although the principal plays an integral role in the school improvement process, getting better is everyone's responsibility. Robert Marzano (2003) concludes that "although it is certainly true that strong leadership from the principal can be a powerful force toward school reform, the notion that an individual can effect change by sheer will and personality is simply not supported by the research" (p. 175). To be substantive, change efforts must be supported by both administrators and teachers. This is possible only when people are working within a strong collaborative culture based on shared values.

> "Sharing the big picture puts everyone on the same page."
>
> —Blanchard and Muchnick (2003, p. 74)

Our emphasis on collaboration does not diminish the importance of a strong principal. On the contrary, we believe that strong formal leadership in a school is essential if improvement is to occur. It is critical that principals make school improvement a priority and that they convey that message to staff. But strong leadership involves sharing responsibility. The principal must start by sharing an overview of the Planning for School and Student Success Process and opening discussion around the notion of planning to improve, not just planning to plan. A related and equally important role for principals is in the creation of an improvement Coordinating Team for the school. By doing these things, principals make a firm statement that they believe in the value of planning for school and student success and, further, that they intend to move forward with supporting the process in their school.

In some schools this approach would be a direct confrontation to the culture. Some staff might object that this "isn't the way things have always been done" or that they are already doing their best or, even worse, might respond with cynical resignation ("This, too, shall pass."). It is important for the principal to understand that there is likely to be resistance and that true change is never easy.

The role of leaders is to positively influence the world of tomorrow through their actions today. To do that, they need to focus on the creation of a culture that is focused on learning and achievement. In the three schools we have highlighted, all of the principals, in their own ways, created such cultures. Each conveyed the message that learning and student achievement were top priorities. Loretta Tetreault at Sacred Heart School said, "I knew not everyone on staff would be on board, as change is difficult, so I braced for the worst and forged ahead." When Irving Jones began to influence the culture at Monticello High School, 25 of the 70 teachers left in the first year. Chris Spence used the phrase "if you can't measure it, you can't improve it" to tell the staff that learning could not be taken for granted. He drew clear boundaries for the staff regarding his position on teamwork and collaboration at Lawrence Heights. Changing a culture from "learning by some" to "learning by all" can be extremely challenging work for everyone involved.

Each of the principals also realized that without staff support it would be impossible to improve the schools. Remember that Loretta Tetreault said, "I will take the credit for initiating the change," but pointed out that "the 'I' very quickly became 'we' when the results of some of our efforts started to show." Chris Spence focused on providing his staff with inspiration and direction as well as support for their improvement efforts. Irving Jones involved the staff in planning and decision-making from the beginning. When faced with a pervasive lack of community trust, the staff of Monticello High School took the bold step of making a public commitment to substantial academic growth over a 3-year period.

> "Leading people is the opposite of trying to control them."
>
> —Blanchard and Muchnick (2003, p. 19)

Leadership for change is not easy nor is it predictable. What can administrators do to create a culture in which leadership is shared, where all members of the community are involved and committed to common goals that focus on learning?

Two Types of Teams for School Improvement

Our belief is that the school planning process needs two different kinds of teams, each with a unique mandate, to accomplish the Planning for School and Student Success Process. The first team, the Coordinating Council, exists to start the process and to support it through to the implementation stage. The second team, the School Success Management Team, takes the reins at that point and sees the process through to the end of the cycle.

The Coordinating Council. This in-house team must be selected carefully to ensure that key stakeholders from the staff are represented without creating a cumbersome group. We believe that the most effective way of forming the Coordinating Council is to involve staff in determining how the school can best be represented and how members should be selected. If the

principal simply appoints people to the council, the staff may see it as just another one of the principal's "good ideas." Typically, councils are composed of representatives of the major divisions in the school and of the school administration. The mandate of this group is to begin the planning process. Since the council includes only a segment of the staff, it will be necessary at this stage to gather input from the rest of the staff, as well as from students, parents, and the community at large in order to get a complete picture of what needs to be done.

The Coordinating Council works best when its sole function is to facilitate the planning process. It is not responsible for creating the plan to improve; instead, its role is to facilitate and support the process. School improvement is a staff issue; the staff should do the planning. Input from parents, students, and other stakeholders is important in the *study* and *reflect* phases of the process; however, the actual work of school improvement falls to the professionals. The Coordinating Council is the most important team in the school. Those who serve on it should be positive people who are passionate about learning and unafraid of change.

Since collaboration and collective decision-making are the keys to success in the planning process, they must be present from the beginning and nurtured continuously through the establishment of professional learning communities. It is important to note that people's ability to function effectively as team members cannot simply be assumed. To expedite the planning process and avoid discouragement, training and professional development will have to be provided at the outset and on an ongoing basis as needs are identified. Training in areas such as collaboration, consensus building, meeting management, data analysis, selection of high-yield strategies, and effective leadership will provide teachers with the tools they need to move forward.

A critical function of the Coordinating Council is to recognize and respect the needs of staff members who are not as committed to the change process as council members. Marzano (2003) suggests that leaders "should be attentive to the concerns of teachers, easily accessible, and should engage in collaborative decision-making and problem-solving with teachers who are not members of the team" (p. 176). Resistance on the part of some staff is to be expected. These staff members may have important insights to offer, and it is important to consider what they have to say. In the final analysis, however, the planning process must proceed. It is also important that dissenters not be viewed as "bad guys." They should continue to be informed and must be supported in understanding the need for change, how it will occur, and what it means for them personally. Schmoker (2001) speaks of leadership as being "defined and actualized through constant, gentle confrontation" for change (p. 21).

The key activity is collaboration. As Lezotte and McKee (2002) point out, "Whoever is not in on what you're doing from the beginning is likely to be down on what you do later" (p. 116). They stress the importance of open two-way communication that ensures that all staff members are knowledgeable about the work of the council and have a chance to offer opinions, ask questions, and express concerns. It is important that agendas for council meetings be distributed to all staff and that the meetings be open to anyone who wishes to attend. When the school plan is formalized, its contents should not be a surprise to anyone.

The change process is messy. It is important to recognize and respect the fact that involving staff in collaborative decision-making and problem-solving is likely to pose challenges when there are varying degrees of commitment to the process. When the principal and Coordinating Council work interdependently with staff, it is difficult for individuals to go unnoticed. Good work is easily noticed and can be celebrated. Those who are not contributing to solutions also stand out. Fullan (2001) reminds us that "there is, in fact, a great deal of peer pressure, along with peer support, in collaborative organizations" (p. 118).

The importance of the principal to the functioning of the Coordinating Council cannot be overstated. When principals consistently deliver the message that they want everyone to feel part of the process, they can work with reluctant staff to ensure that opting out is not an alternative. A large part of the principal's role is to anticipate the barriers to success and plan for ways to overcome them.

The School Success Management Team. During implementation (phase 5), a team with a different purpose needs to be activated. The School Success Management Team is intended to support and monitor the implementation of plans that have been developed during earlier phases.

We have chosen the term "management" deliberately to reinforce the notion that any change must be managed if it is to become embedded in a new culture. A school that commits to improvement is committing to a long-term process. This team's job is to facilitate the work and keep the commitment alive. If the change process is not managed, there is a good likelihood that new ideas will give way to old familiar ways.

The School Success Management Team is ideally a microcosm of the school community. It may include staff, student, and parent representatives; personnel from the central office; and representatives from the broader community. It is conceivable that teachers who worked on the Coordinating Council might remain to serve on the team; however, new teacher representatives could also become involved at this point.

The mandate of the School Success Management Team is to support the work of the professional learning communities. To that end, representatives from each PLC should attend regular meetings with the team to share their work and tell about progress being made toward the accomplishment of their goals. This would be a time for celebration and for "in-flight correction" as the team collaborates with members of the PLCs to move the improvement process forward.

The team should keep in mind that better results may not be realized instantly. In fact, it may be some time before the impact of new strategies and processes is actually recognized. A consistent finding about the change process in education is that all successful schools experience what Michael Fullan (2001) calls the "implementation dip." The implementation dip is characterized by a decline in performance and confidence as people encounter situations that require new skills and new understandings.

New innovations place people in situations where they are called upon to change their behavior and alter their beliefs. The discomfort that comes from being in this position may result in people feeling anxious, fearful, confused, and overwhelmed. They may begin to question their own competence and be tempted to retreat to the "old way" of doing things. Hence, an implementation dip occurs. Support, encouragement,

and celebration of achievements to date become doubly important when this occurs. The School Success Management Team has a large role to play in keeping the change process moving forward.

These dips are understandable. People go through transition as they come to grips with change. For some this transition is a long and painful process. Others embrace change and manage transitions relatively easily. William Bridges (1991) points out that the old way of doing things will always overpower the new way if the new way does not have ongoing support. "It isn't the changes that do you in," he explains, "it's the transitions" (p. 3). The School Success Management Team must be sensitive to such responses and provide the necessary support to keep the change process moving forward.

An effective School Success Management Team knows that change is a process, not an event. Members of the team understand about the implementation dip and do not panic when there are glitches in the implementation of new strategies or processes. They are empathic and supportive toward the people immersed in the work. The team is charged with the responsibility of keeping the change process alive.

Each school year, the culminating activity of the School Success Management Team is to prepare and present a report on the Planning for School and Student Success Process to the community. The information included in this report provides a foundation for the next year's planning.

Summary

Local, state, or provincial legislation in some locations will specifically require that parents, students, and members of the community be involved in all phases of the planning process. If this is the case, the Coordinating Council would remain in place throughout.

We believe, however, that the existence of two discrete bodies—the Coordinating Council and the School Success Management Team—can benefit the planning process. Our experience has been that when the process is begun by a Coordinating Council composed of their colleagues, teachers feel more comfortable, speak more openly, and set more demanding goals. We believe that team development is enhanced if the planning is "owned" by those who will be doing the work.

Having both authority and responsibility for studying, reflecting, planning, and implementing allows teachers the professional latitude to tailor the school plan to meet the goals they identify, through review of critical evidence, as being most important. Since this planning process is based on continuous improvement, it should be reviewed, and if necessary revised, each year to ensure that it is meeting school needs. There may come a time when only one team is required; however, we contend that the decision about when that should happen is best left to the professionals who are doing the improvement work at the school.

The importance of leadership in the school improvement process cannot be overstated. We believe that effective leadership for change is characterized by commitment, tenacity, optimism, and strong, respectful relationships. Moral purpose and hope provide a solid foundation for the efforts of leaders in the change process. This chapter has outlined two team structures that can facilitate and promote the school improvement process. In effective schools, leadership does not belong to just one person. It is shared and as a result, its beneficial impact is multiplied.

Leadership is about direction. Leaders influence others to take positive action. In the next chapter, we introduce phase 1, "set the course," of the Planning for School and Student Success Process. Since it establishes direction, we see it as a vital leadership component of the process.

Set the Course

(Values, Vision, Purpose)

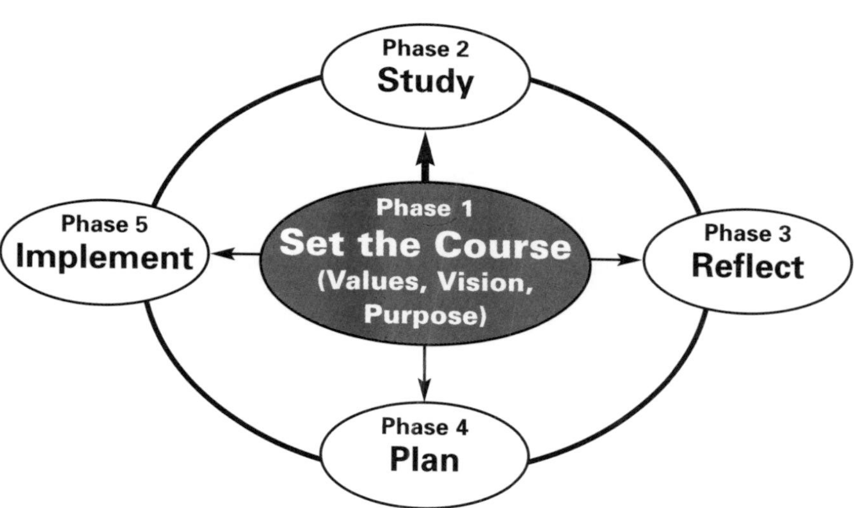

Phase 1 in the Planning for School and Student Success Process is the articulation of a school's values, vision, and purpose. This process is at the core or heart of the planning process. Values, vision, and purpose are the foundation of the school's culture and are crucial to the kind of purposeful optimism that characterizes Harbors of Hope.

Values First—Then Vision and Purpose

Practical experience and many years of working with school staffs have taught us that shared values must be identified before a statement of vision is created. We have also learned that "purpose" might be a better term than "mission" for use at the school level. Vision statements are a projection of values, an articulation of how those values will look in action. The purpose statement identifies what is most valued. Because values form the foundation for both vision and purpose, we place them first in the process.

We realize that this position is not aligned with much of the current literature on organizational excellence. The usual recommendation is to begin by creating a mission statement that establishes the reason for the organization's existence. According to that plan, the vision statement comes next and creates a picture of the ideal future. Last are values statements, which outline the behaviors that will be required if the vision is to be fulfilled.

We recommend the opposite process for schools because we believe that behaviors are influenced by values. When we value kindness, we act kindly. When we value safety, we take safety precautions. If teachers value parents as partners, they will work to communicate with them in ways that are open and honest.

Experience has shown us that when staffs create statements of core values, they focus on the emotional side of education. The process reminds them of the importance of their work and engages their hearts. In focusing on the identification of core values, we are asking educators to think about what really matters in their work. When teachers commit to valuing learning and student achievement, they will search for ways to enhance

both. A school's values provide the criteria for asking the questions and searching for the answers that will make a difference to school culture and student achievement. Vision statements express what the school would look like if the values were being lived every day. The statement of purpose is intended to capture the emotion and commitment in a simple, inspiring statement.

Why Purpose Instead of Mission?

Most organizations have spent a lot of time creating mission statements. These statements are intended to describe the purpose of the organization. Our experience has been that the time spent fine-tuning a mission statement would be better used in clarifying the purpose of the school or organization.

Webster defines a mission as "a commission or special assignment given to a person or group." If the mission is considered to embody the values and vision of the organization, then each staff member should be expected to accept the "commission," and in so doing would be viewed as empowered. Experience has shown us, however, that teachers as professionals prefer to have some control over their futures and their actions. For that reason, we do not believe that schools benefit from spending their time developing a mission statement. We recommend instead that they articulate their statement of purpose.

Purpose, according to Webster's dictionary, is "intention, resolution, determination." It is also "an anticipated outcome that is intended or that guides your planned action" as well as being "the quality of being determined to do or achieve something." Lezotte and McKee (2002) assert that "there is a world of difference between having a mission statement and having a *sense of mission*" (p. 119). As we see it, a purpose statement reflects the "sense of mission" shared by those who create it. We feel that "purpose" is a word that more adequately captures the intention of the process for schools. It is important that a school's statement of purpose be aligned with the ideals embodied in the mission of the school district or government. As schools work toward meeting their individual purpose, they are contributing to the realization of the mission of the district or government.

Expecting professional staff to accept a "commission" is looking for compliance with the mission statement. A school that creates a purpose statement that grows from what the staff cares about has a greater chance of gaining commitment. After all, we can legislate and supervise for compliance, but commitment is a personal gift given by inspired professionals. Statements of purpose are more simply stated as well as more representative of the hope and passion brought to the teaching profession by the individuals who create them.

Creating change in schools is hard work. This work involves the heart and commitment, not just the head and compliance. It is not possible to mandate change, only compliance. This is why values form the foundation of school improvement, as shown in the pyramid on the next page, followed by vision and purpose.

Typically, a staff will develop a number of statements that reflect their values and vision before they feel prepared to synthesize their thinking and articulate their purpose statement. In some of the most aligned schools we have known, individual teachers have extended this process to create their personal values, vision, and purpose statements, which they then post for students and classroom visitors to see.

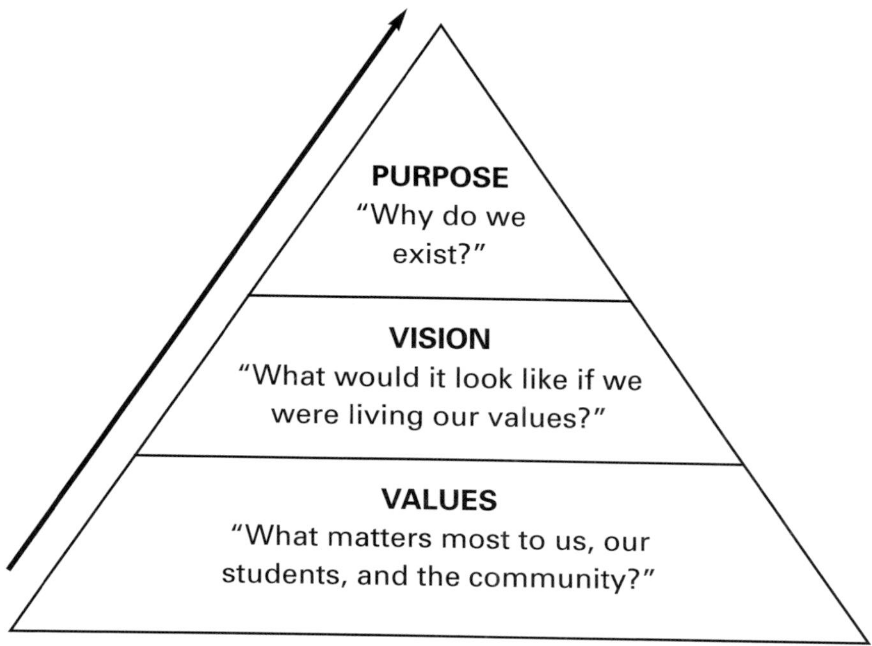

The following set of questions is a very simple version of the discussion questions that can help a school staff create meaningful statements intended to inspire them as they commit to the Planning for School and Student Success Process.

Values

Q: What matters most to us, our students, and the community?

A: We value student success.

Vision

Q: What would our school look like if we were living this value?

A: We would teach in ways that engage students and would create strategies to support all students so that they could meet with success.

Purpose

Q: Why do we exist?

A: Our purpose is to create hope by ensuring success for all students.

Phase 1, the "set the course" component of the Planning for School and Student Success Process, does not require a great deal of time. One professional day would be sufficient to involve the entire staff in generating the foundational ideas. The work done during that day could be fine-tuned by the Coordinating Council, and the final statements could then be presented to the staff for affirmation. Many planning processes are derailed as a result of long days spent creating a mission statement that says very little that is meaningful or inspiring to the staff.

Summary

Efforts to develop a statement of core **values** will not move a school into the future by themselves. Discussing core values will, however, help a school staff reflect about what matters most to them. This reflection will lead to statements of **vision** that answer the question, "What would our school look like if we were living our values?" A **purpose** statement captures the feelings and thoughts embedded in the values and vision statements. It is simple enough for everyone to remember and clear enough to be instantly understood as guidance.

Schools improve as a result of changes in behaviors, not simply because a school has articulated value, vision, and purpose statements. The real value of the work done in phase 1, "set the course," is the establishment of direction for the entire school improvement process. With the direction clear, the staff is ready to assess how their present level of performance measures up.

They need to study how they are doing on what they have said matters.

When a school's values, vision, and purpose are understood by all, critical evidence can be gathered in ways that allow the staff to see how they are doing at achieving the things they value the most. Their reflection on this information allows for the creation of professional learning communities that develop and implement plans to improve outcomes in areas that have been identified as crucial. When educators work in this way, they use the values, vision, and purpose statements to focus their school improvement efforts.

Chapter 6

Study

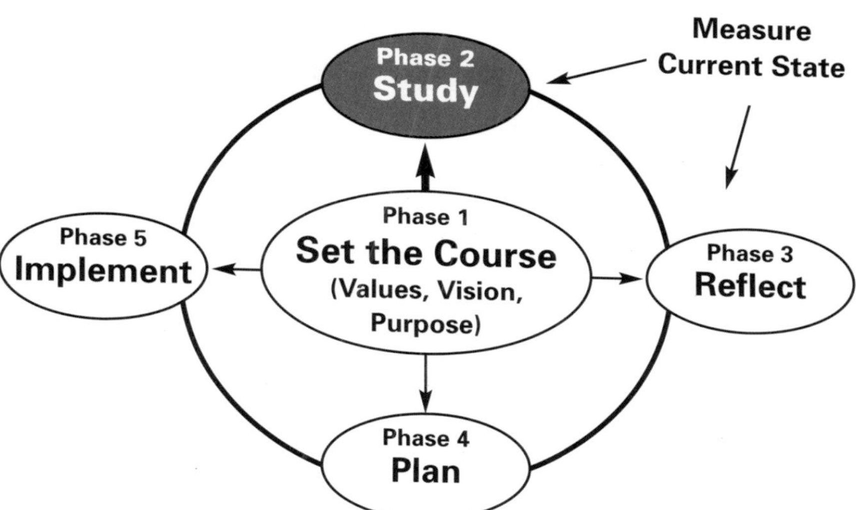

The study involved in phase 2 is a critical activity in the Planning for School and Student Success Process. If the planning process is to yield real improvement, the study phase must be approached with care. The important questions must be asked, and critical evidence must be gathered to answer them. As we indicated earlier, we believe that "critical evidence" is a more accurate term than "data" for the information that a school staff needs to gather and examine. There is such an abundance of data available in schools that years could be spent manipulating it while devoting no time to action and achieving no measurable progress in any area. Our intention in using the term "critical evidence" is to convey the idea that the data gathered are data that matter. Both qualitative and quantitative data are valuable as long as they provide information on things that matter.

Measure what matters!

Avoid analysis paralysis!

Lezotte and McKee (2002) tell us that it is important that schools are "explicit and intentional about what they plan to measure and monitor" in order to honor their values and meet their goals (p. 145). Marzano (2003) calls the collection of critical evidence "taking the pulse" of the school (p. 160). Change is a slow, often messy process that occurs differently in response to the context within which it is happening. It is important that critical evidence be used to inform actions as well as to evaluate the impact of those actions.

Critical Evidence

Critical evidence includes test scores, of course, but also much more. Quantitative and qualitative data are both important. Any kind of data that can offer insight into how effectively a school is educating its students is data that could be critical evidence. This evidence can come from students, parents, staff, or the broader community. Test scores and other forms of academic assessment are only part of this evidence. Just as important is information on classroom achievement, attendance, behavior, and attitude, as well as any other observations that a school staff believes will be useful to their investigations. We

stress *measuring what matters*, which means that the critical factor is not the assessment tool, but its interpreter. In schools that are striving to become Harbors of Hope, where staff members are empowered and involved in gathering critical evidence, all kinds of data are considered.

Not everyone will be enthusiastic about gathering critical evidence. Past experience and the pass-fail mindsets in schools may cause staff to resist the gathering of data. Some may actually want to avoid facing clear evidence of the impact of their work with students. District, state, provincial, or national measures, along with the notion of accountability, may evoke defensive or dismissive responses from teachers. An expectation that they streamline and reflect on school-based assessment may also be resisted.

Threatened by the prospect of what critical evidence might tell them, some educators may be inclined to use it to rationalize the current performance of the school and the students. Some may dismiss evidence as unimportant because they are unsure about how to use and interpret it. For others, the use of critical evidence represents new ways of thinking and working that they find uncomfortable and would rather avoid. Some may be suspicious that the information will be used to evaluate or judge their performance as teachers. Many teachers will find ways to avoid using critical evidence to guide their work with students. Those teachers, sadly, are missing the opportunity to use a rich source of information that will have a powerful impact on the achievement of their students as well as on their own professional practice.

Stephen Covey (1989) points out the difference between proactive and reactive responses to the world around us. Reactive people or organizations tend to absolve themselves of responsibility by blaming others. In the educational context, it is easy to blame "them"—administrators and others who set standards and create policies. Proactive people or organizations, however, do not dwell on what they cannot control. Instead they focus their energies on what they can change or influence. They take a hopeful stance and optimistically forge ahead. We believe that the Planning for School and Student Success Process offers an opportunity for educators to be proactive in their work with children. When educators accept that critical evidence is a tool to assist them in their work and to track progress over a period of years, the real work of school improvement can begin.

Many things should be considered when collecting and studying the various sources of critical evidence available to educators. We believe that not all schools will achieve at the same rate, but all schools can improve. In addition, we believe that the students who show up each day are the best children their parents have, and our responsibility is to help them learn in a culture of hope. When schools focus on improvement, they gather critical evidence to establish where they are currently. Once collected, such evidence can be addressed proactively as plans are developed to improve student performance. This proactive approach is the difference between schools that "plan to plan" and schools that "plan to improve."

Mandated Testing

Over the years, there has been so much dissension about provincial- and state-mandated testing that we believe a fundamental reality has been ignored. The reality is that curricula and guidelines that come from the government are the outcomes of extensive collaboration to determine what students

need to know and be able to do upon graduation. As Lezotte and McKee (2002) tell us, "the state standards comprise the 'floor' or minimum standards that schools must embrace" (p. 133). The same is true with Canadian provincial standards. Furthermore, once the state or provincial standards are understood, local districts are free to collaborate with their stakeholders to add the standards they feel are missing. The bottom line, however, is that state and provincial standards cannot be ignored or eliminated. Nor should they be. They are developed by educators and grounded in research about the skills and attitudes students will need to prepare for the future.

DuFour and Eaker (1998) point out that national, state or provincial, or district curriculum frameworks "can serve as excellent resources in the investigation of curriculum" and that "teachers are likely to find that there is little with which they disagree when they take the time to analyze these frameworks" (p. 154).

We are not implying that educators should proceed passively in their use of assessments or should avoid speaking out against wrongheaded or unfair assessment items or practices. Schmoker (2000) quotes Fullan as saying "Go to the danger" (p. 64). He is speaking expressly of mandated testing as well as accountability systems. We are cautioned to have a fair regard for the fact that, warts and all, these assessment and accountability systems establish the context for improvement. Schmoker emphasizes the importance of learning how to use the information gleaned from these tests and accountability systems, and the importance of preparing students for taking the tests so that they can show what they know and have a fair chance of succeeding.

It is important to remember that provincial and state assessments are just one source of critical evidence about student achievement. While they can provide valuable guidance for instruction and school improvement efforts, there are numerous other means of assessment that are also useful and that should be used in order to obtain a comprehensive picture of student achievement and instructional needs. The fact that government assessments are administered only at certain grade levels poses a dilemma for teachers at other grade levels, who may want more information about how their students are doing, or which areas are in greatest need of attention. Schmoker (2001) believes that the solutions to this dilemma are locally developed assessments that focus on "the most essential learnings" that have been identified by teachers through vertical and horizontal curriculum mapping. Locally developed assessment tools are a rich source of data that can be used to determine instructional goals for students as well as evaluate learning outcomes. An advantage of such assessment tools is that their development requires in-depth teacher understanding of curriculum as well as reflection on desired student outcomes.

> If everything is important, then nothing is important.
>
> —Grant Wiggins (1998, p. 179)

Measures of an Effective School (Achievement, Attendance, Attitude, and Behavior)

Effective Schools researchers note that student achievement, attendance, attitudes, and behavior are the most powerful indicators used in their research. These four indicators are deeply interconnected. Student attendance influences achievement. Negative attitudes engender poor behavior, and poorly behaved

students are often removed from class or suspended from school. When attendance suffers, achievement declines.

Four Indicators of Success

- Achievement
- Attendance
- Attitudes
- Behavior

Which of the four indicators matters the most? Some would say that attitude is the most important. We agree that it is very important, but feel that it is necessary to ask, "How can students maintain a positive attitude if they are failing in their learning?" Students who are not successfully learning will almost always be the poorest attendees, the most difficult to manage, and very often the most negative about school. Most children begin their school careers with excitement about their futures. Sadly, however, by the third grade many are beginning to fall behind in their learning. When a student is unsuccessful, his or her self-image as a learner takes a serious hit and the cycle of deteriorating attendance, behavior, and attitude begins. Achievement is the key to keeping students coming to school, feeling positive about themselves as learners, and behaving in ways that sustain their success.

The "Learning for All—Whatever It Takes" mission of effective schools suggests that student achievement is reflected by a variety of what Lezotte and McKee (2002) call "output measures." Such measures would include state or provincial assessment scores, end-of-course assessments, classroom-based assessments and any other indicators that provide evidence of achievement. Lezotte and McKee maintain that "no school or district can be judged as effective . . . if it cannot demonstrate high student achievement in the essential curriculum as reflected in output measures without major gaps in the distribution of achievement across the various student groups" (p. 22). The student groups they mention are identified by gender, race or ethnicity, and socioeconomic status. Effective schools do what it takes to close the achievement gaps that exist between groups of students. Their focus is equity and learning for all.

Critical Evidence: Measuring What Matters

Staff members may gather critical evidence from a variety of sources in a variety of ways. The important questions to ask are, "Does this evidence give us information on what we value?" and "Are we measuring what matters?" Experience and discussion with numerous schools across North America have allowed us to summarize our observations about using critical evidence to have maximum impact on school and student success as follows:

- Critical evidence provides baseline data for the planning process. It also provides formative and summative information for instruction (assessment *for* and *of* learning).
- The critical evidence collected in one school year becomes the baseline data for the next year's Planning for School and Student Success Process.
- Critical evidence is value-free until it is interpreted. Then it becomes information to be used for planning purposes. Plans are influenced by what the staff has said it values.

- The human dimensions of a school cannot be captured using numbers; therefore, both qualitative and quantitative critical evidence should be gathered.
- Numbers and measurement (quantitative data) are vital descriptors of the static dimensions of a school. Feedback from people, based on their experience and perceptions (qualitative data), contributes to a view of the dynamic human dimensions.
- The process of gathering and interpreting critical evidence is as important as the actual planning and implementation.
- Everyone who could be affected by the collection and use of critical evidence should be involved in influencing the process and outcomes.

A Continuing Cycle of Improvement

In the Planning for School and Student Success Process, staff members begin by identifying their shared values. The process continues when staff gathers critical evidence to determine how they are doing on what they say matters most (their shared values). Through interpretation and reflection, the staff identifies areas in need of improvement. As part of the planning process, staff working in professional learning communities set goals and select high-yield strategies to help them meet the goals. As the strategies are implemented, the process is monitored through the periodic collection of more critical evidence. This new critical evidence either validates the work being done or indicates what needs to be adjusted.

Each of the three schools we highlight throughout this book is unique. Sacred Heart is a small inner-city school that serves a

Critical Evidence and Planning

- Schools establish goals based on what they value.
- Structures and processes are implemented to support staff efforts to reach their goals.
- The collection and analysis of critical evidence helps schools determine whether their declared values are being honored.
- Critical evidence is used in ongoing assessment of progress in enhancing student achievement.

large aboriginal population on the Canadian prairies. Lawrence Heights is a middle school that serves inner-city students in Toronto, while Monticello is located in rural Virginia and serves a diverse population of high school students. Although the schools differ in many respects, the work of all three led to improvement in student achievement, attendance, behavior, and attitudes. Staff at these schools began planning from a values perspective and studied their schools by collecting critical evidence that became the basis for setting goals and taking action.

Consider Monticello High School. From the beginning, the staff there was committed to two pervasive values, which they expressed in the statements: "Kids come first," and "To teach them, you have to reach them." They went public with their commitment to reach the state standard in 4 years. In 1998–1999, the staff reviewed math scores for 233 ninth-grade students and found they had a percentile ranking of 48. They gathered data in a way that allowed them to disaggregate it on the basis on gender and race. By setting specific goals and altering their practice,

they made remarkable strides. In 3 years the overall performance of ninth-grade students had increased by 15% and the performance of the African-American student population had increased by 20%. They began by studying information on the current situation and used it to establish focused goals and implement new structures and systems for enhancing student achievement. They closed the gender and race performance gaps through gathering and tracking critical evidence as they employed high-yield strategies in their work with students. All of their efforts were responsive to their stated values.

Summary

Study is crucial to the planning process. Beginning with a set of core values, a school can tailor its data-gathering to meet its needs. “Measuring what matters” involves defining what matters through the identification of shared values and then the creation or selection of assessment tools that will provide critical evidence that can be used in planning to improve. Reflection on the critical evidence gathered will inform subsequent actions to be taken on the journey toward becoming a Harbor of Hope.

Reflect

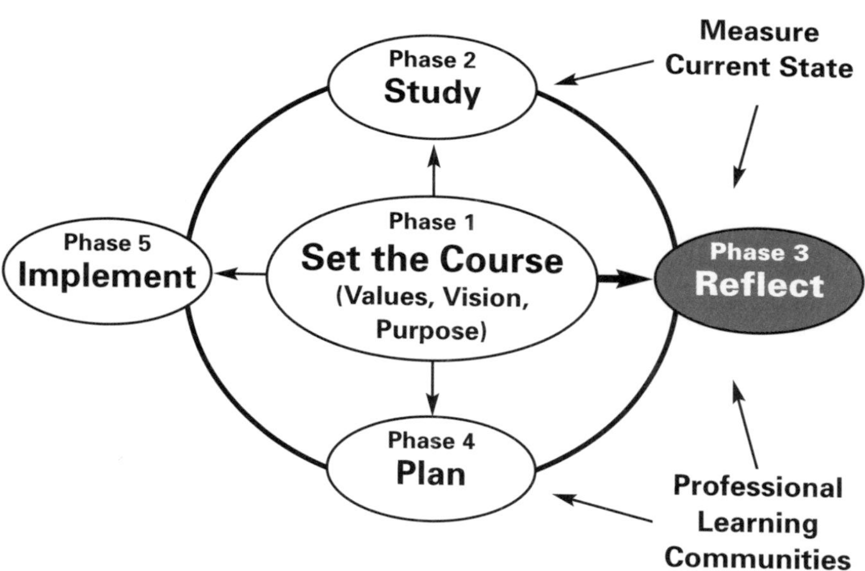

Phase 3, a period of reflection, is essential to the Planning for School and Student Success Process. It is a chance for all involved to weigh evidence that has been gathered and organized during the study phase. If the study phase has been done well, the reflect phase will not require a great deal of time.

As always, the key activity is collaboration. It is important that the entire staff review the collected critical evidence in order to gain a global perspective on the current state of the school's performance. For example, tracking literacy and numeracy achievement through the grades may reveal obvious points at which students encounter difficulty. Shared perspectives and collaboration between teachers at different levels are helpful to identify issues, to understand students, and to plan instruction that will meet their learning needs so that progress can be made. This process offers an opportunity for the staff to gain a "big picture" awareness of the interdependence between all divisions and grades within the school.

The reflect phase is most powerful when the critical evidence can be disaggregated in meaningful ways. Disaggregation is the process of analyzing data for distinct subgroups. For example, we may want to disaggregate attendance data by gender. We might also want to relate attendance patterns to learning outcomes. It is important not to bury staff members in meaningless data but rather to give them an opportunity to explore critical evidence that will prompt insights into the performance patterns of students and the impact of their instructional practice. Disaggregation helps with such exploration.

The Importance of Disaggregation

Consider the following four levels of critical evidence from a school with students from grades one through six and the observations for each level.

Level 1—Overall School Results in Reading

On the district test of reading administered at all grade levels during May, the average performance level for the school was at 58%.

Observation: This information is quite general and does not hold much promise for grade or student specific planning. It could, however, generate a discussion about whether overall achievement at the 58th percentile is considered adequate for the school.

Level 2—Overall School Results Disaggregated by Gender

On the district test of reading administered during May, the average performance level for the school by gender was 66% for girls and 50% for boys.

Observation: These numbers indicate a large discrepancy in general achievement levels between girls and boys. This is important information.

Level 3—Disaggregation by Grade

The scores are reported by average percentile ranking.

Grade	1	2	3	4	5	6
Scores	63%	64%	59%	56%	51%	49%

Observation: This information indicates that, on the whole, students begin to encounter more difficulty in the third grade. This critical evidence could prompt staff to explore the causes and look for appropriate interventions.

Level 4—Disaggregation by Grade and Gender

The scores are reported by average percentile ranking.

Grade	1	2	3	4	5	6
Grade Average	63%	64%	59%	56%	51%	49%
Boys	63%	63%	57%	52%	42%	44%
Girls	63%	65%	61%	60%	60%	54%

Observation: The critical evidence here substantiates what was indicated in level 2. Boys experience more difficulty with reading, and grade three seems to be where the achievement gap becomes most apparent.

In looking at critical evidence, it is important to remember that the results obtained are the outcome of the work done by all staff up to and including the grade being studied. For example, the grade six results are not solely the responsibility of the sixth-grade teachers but are a concern for the entire staff from grade one onward. This is also important information for the teachers who will be working with these students beginning in grade seven.

Disaggregation helps the staff reflect on critical evidence and is intended for planning and monitoring over both the short term and the long term. It is a problem-finding strategy—a powerful process, since every successful problem-solving endeavor begins with an accurate description of the problem.

Obvious discrepancies will be apparent when the staff reflects to compare what they have said they value with the critical evidence that is in front of them. The questions then become, "Why are we seeing this?" and "What can we do about it?" It is important that the entire staff understand the "big picture" in terms of the school's current performance; however, the real power of the critical evidence is realized when the staff begins to associate the data they study with their own work with their students. It is at this point in the planning process that we recommend the formation of learning teams to explore the problems in more depth and to begin to collaborate on finding solutions.

Collaborative Reflection: Professional Learning Communities

> "The most promising strategy for sustained, substantive school improvement is building the capacity of school personnel to function as a professional learning community."
>
> —DuFour and Eaker (1998, p. 129).

Modern organizations have come to understand that collaboration and continuous learning are the vehicles for success. Peter Senge (1990) had a major impact on organizations when he declared that "the most successful corporation of the future will be a learning organization" (p. 4). Peter Drucker (1992) added that "every enterprise has to become a learning institution [and] a teaching institution. Organizations that build in continuous learning in jobs will dominate the twenty-first century" (p. 108). Robert Marzano (2003) discovered that one of the five school-level factors for success is "staff collegiality and professionalism." Newmann and Wehlage (1995) probably made the most powerful statement about the importance of professional learning communities in schools when they observed, "If schools want to enhance their organizational capacity to boost student learning, they should work on building a professional community that is characterized by shared purpose, collaborative activity, and collective responsibility among staff" (p. 37). The evidence is clear that to accomplish and sustain improvement efforts, all members of the organization need to be involved in the key activity: collaboration.

Structuring the Professional Learning Community

As we explain in chapter 2, we see the entire staff of a school district as a large professional learning community within which smaller groupings of people also function as professional learning communities with different focus areas. All staff members in the school district are part of three configurations of the PLC: small professional learning community "teams," and school-wide and district-level professional learning communities. Each PLC works collaboratively in different ways toward the goal of achieving success with all students. We believe that our perception of how professional learning communities function is aligned with the characteristics of effective PLCs that are identified by DuFour and Eaker (1998), listed on the next page, and described in this chapter.

The key to professional learning communities is that they be composed of a group of teachers collaborating to set goals and to plan and implement the structures and processes that will enhance individual student or whole school success. Members of PLCs share a common purpose and can create more flexibility for learning when they work together.

In our view, professional learning communities can have a variety of configurations, such as:

- Teachers of the same grade
- Interdisciplinary groups of teachers who share the same group of students
- Teachers who have common professional development goals
- Teachers who teach the same subjects
- Teachers working together on a common school-wide goal

Through reflection on the critical evidence gathered in phase 2, staff members can collaborate to identify the areas requiring improvement. Three questions are pertinent for guiding their reflection:

1. What does the critical evidence tell us about areas that need to be improved?
2. What areas, if improved, would have the greatest impact on student learning?
3. What exactly would we like to improve in the identified areas?

Reflection on these questions helps to clarify the critical evidence and idea sharing and lays the groundwork for the formal goal setting that will guide the planning process. The goals will focus on those aspects of the school's culture that have the greatest potential to make a positive difference for students and learning.

Characteristics of Effective PLCs

(Adapted from DuFour and Eaker, 1998)

- Collaborative mindset
- Focus on learning
- Focus on results
- Orientation toward action
- Collective inquiry
- Timely, relevant information
- Commitment to continuous improvement

The Power of Professional Learning Communities

To meet the challenge of "Learning for All—Whatever It Takes," staff members are required to work in new ways that change the culture of the school by altering "the way we do things around here." By collaborating and reflecting in professional learning communities, a school staff will acquire new understandings about teaching and develop new attitudes toward the learning process. Old paradigms about education will be shaken, new ones will be created, and the culture of the school will shift as shown in the feature box below. These shifts may be significant and result in tension for many staff members. An environment of collaboration and teamwork will allow staff to support and encourage each other in the transition.

PLCs Shift School Culture

From		To
Teaching	➡	Learning
Teacher isolation	➡	Collaboration
Pass/fail mindset	➡	Elimination of failure
Compliance	➡	Commitment
Curriculum overload	➡	Guaranteed curriculum
General goals	➡	Specific goals
Static assessment	➡	Dynamic assessment
Over-the-wall grade promotions	➡	Flexible structures
Planning to plan	➡	Planning to improve
Time and staff fixed	➡	Learning fixed
Learning for most	➡	Learning for all

The Role of PLCs in Shifting School Culture

From teaching to learning. The old paradigm for schools focused on teaching. Today, the focus is on learning. The question for teachers is not "Did I cover the curriculum?" but rather, "Did the students achieve the essential learning?" Answers to this question will provide the information teachers need as they proceed with their planning. Teachers as well as students are learners in this process. In the past, supervision was used to check that teachers were teaching properly. Today, supervision focuses on accountability for improved results, with coaching and support offered to teachers as they work to create conditions that will bring students to higher levels of achievement.

From teacher isolation to collaboration. Schools that continue to operate in the old paradigm sustain the industrial model that was current in the 1940s and 1950s. In that model, teachers work in isolation, making independent decisions on teaching, assessment, and reporting strategies. In that model, schools are organized according to class size and grade level, and grades are organized according to student age. Teachers and their classes function as islands.

Schools that embrace the notion of collaboration and shared leadership recognize that when teachers work together, student learning improves. Schmoker (2001) tells us that "true collaboration is a discipline—a fragile, high-maintenance set of practices and attitudes that need constant care and attention" (p. 11). He explains that leadership is the key to developing and nurturing professional learning communities that then form the foundation for a collaborative school culture:

> Without a formal schedule or an explicit commitment to a result, collaboration devolves into just another option

> or mere talk. Focused, professional interaction is an unnatural activity. The potential for drift and delay is everywhere. To compel energy and attendance, leaders must schedule, monitor and focus teamwork on an explicit, measurable result. (p. 11)

In this way, our key activity, collaboration, activates our key concept, purposeful hope.

From a pass/fail mindset to eliminating failure. Schools that function in the old paradigm still believe it is their job to sort students and direct them to various programs based on their ability as determined by their teachers. When schools are organized according to class size and grade with students organized according to their age, students pass or fail grades depending upon how successfully they complete the work of each grade. In this structure, the individual learner gets lost and the gap in achievement levels widens as students progress through the grades. When teachers have students in their classrooms with skill levels spanning several years, the task of addressing learning needs becomes very complex and the result is often discouragement on the part of both students and teachers.

To meet the needs of their students, teachers need to be able to identify and understand differing learning styles and the impact of emotion on the ability to learn. Daniel Goleman (1995) tells us that the development of emotional intelligence is hugely affected by poverty, broken families, and the lack of school success. Schools can do nothing about the socioeconomic or family status of their students; they can, however, do a lot about the conditions for learning while students are at school. The students who do not fit the "one grade per year" mold require an environment that allows continuous progress in

recognition of their need for more time and additional, differentiated instruction to achieve the baseline outcomes. A pass/fail system for these students does nothing more than discourage and alienate. Effective schools provide the structures and supports required to improve the learning outcomes for all students and eliminate large achievement gaps.

From compliance to commitment. Another throwback to the industrial model of education still exists in the belief that results can be improved by creating rules, guidelines, and monitoring structures to cover any situation that might arise in a school. This kind of thinking is predicated on the assumption that fairness requires that everyone must behave and be treated the same way. Detailed policy and procedures manuals are developed to convey the rules and structures thought to be necessary if schools are to function effectively. We recognize now that those manuals and all the rules they represent are symptomatic of a lack of trust and a demand for compliance. Compliant following of rules results in a culture that stifles passion and creativity. People in rule-ridden organizations are often cynical and inclined to work to the lowest acceptable level. They may wonder why they should go the extra mile, considering that their efforts will be neither recognized nor valued.

Commitment is a gift given to schools by individuals. Staff members determine their individual level of commitment depending upon how they feel about their work. In a culture that inspires commitment by valuing learning and innovation, people are encouraged to take the risks required to develop new competencies, achieve new insights, and reach new heights in their professional lives.

Those who work in a culture demanding compliance see teaching as a job. Those who work in a culture that inspires commitment see it as a calling. The champions in education are those who make a commitment to schools, learning, and students. They go the extra mile because they believe they can make a difference and they accept the fact that improving a school is hard work.

From curriculum overload to guaranteed curriculum. Teachers today are faced with curricula that are extremely demanding. They struggle with having limited time to "deliver" curricula filled with expectations that are virtually impossible to meet with students characterized by a wide range of abilities. If they are to get a grip on these enormous issues, teachers must be able to identify which curricular outcomes are "essential" or "baseline." At the same time, they must study instructional practice to ensure that they employ only the most powerful learning strategies.

Teachers working in collaborative teams can study curriculum to develop skill development sequences, or continua, that identify baseline outcomes for *all* students in all disciplines. They can also identify the outcomes that *most* students will achieve and go on to identify those appropriate for students who *consistently exceed expectations*. By mapping curriculum both vertically (up the grades) and horizontally (between disciplines), it is possible to determine the "guaranteed curriculum" and to plan for addressing the varying abilities of all students. This work requires new priorities for teacher time and a new understanding of professional development. (The notion of aligned curriculum is developed more completely in chapter 9.)

From general goals to specific goals. In many districts, the senior administration identifies system goals that are expected to apply to all schools. They are usually broadly stated and are goals worth striving for. Often, however, these goals do not have meaning for teachers because teachers have not been involved in creating them. DuFour and Eaker (1998) observe that "teachers recognize the inherent unfairness of a system that asks them to be accountable for results, but provides them with little or no opportunity to make the decisions that affect those results." They refute the notion that board members and administrators must "make the decisions because they are responsible for the consequences," pointing out that the relevant question is not "Who is in charge?" but rather, "How can we best get results?" They believe that the answer to that question "lies in empowering teachers through collaborative processes that provide them with authority that is commensurate to their responsibility" (p. 153).

While it is important that teacher, school, and district goals be aligned, the nuances of goals set must be school- and teacher-specific to be meaningful. Teachers, given the professional latitude that is their due, will collaborate to establish and commit to goals based on their study of the critical evidence pertaining to their school and students. Those who set the goals should be accountable for the results achieved. Professional learning communities provide an important structure within which this collaboration can occur.

From static to dynamic assessment. Static assessment is used in isolation, usually to obtain marks that can be used in reporting. Dynamic assessment, on the other hand, is used to inform and monitor the learning process. It is cyclical and ongoing, focusing on identifying the areas where students are struggling and then on assessing the effectiveness of learning activities that are provided to address areas of difficulty. Dynamic assessment is a powerful tool for tracking student achievement and for informing the next instructional steps. It helps teachers identify learning styles and needs. Use of dynamic assessment allows schools to know generally how their students are growing from year to year as well as how specific cohorts of students are progressing.

Competency in collecting and using assessment information is the most important set of skills teachers can develop. When teachers are skilled at using assessment information in their daily work, the result is effective instruction for all students that will lead to higher scores on provincial or state standards tests. External test results will take care of themselves when all students benefit from accurate local assessment and appropriate instruction to facilitate their achievement in the essential outcomes.

Working as part of a professional learning community, teachers have the opportunity to collaborate to examine student progress and plan for appropriate instruction at all levels. Professional learning communities offer the potential for peer support, shared responsibility, and the creation of flexible structures to support the learning of all students.

From "over the wall" to flexible structures. Each spring, teachers who work in "over the wall" schools develop classroom groupings of predetermined size and throw their students "over the wall" to next year's teacher. Classes are established based on "technical" formulas provided by central office and "learner characteristic" formulas developed by staff. Thus third-grade teachers throw their students to the fourth-grade teachers, who are themselves busily throwing students to the fifth-grade teach-

ers. This is a bureaucratic structure that assumes that every student is ready to be thrown at the same time. It is a convenient way to organize but is very ineffective for learning.

As schools and systems reconcile themselves to the realization that many students do not fit into neat "boxes," we are confident that flexible structures will be developed to accommodate the varying learning needs of students. If flexible structures are to be effective, teachers must be willing to think differently about how they work, and districts must be willing to support any needed changes.

An example of a flexible structure that has been successful is multi-grading, which involves teachers having more than one grade level in a single classroom. The multi-grade classroom is highly valued by those who see the potential that exists in such settings for continuous progress and cross-age learning. The unique grade groupings at Sacred Heart School have proven so successful that the only "single-grade" classroom that presently exists there is kindergarten. The Sacred Heart teachers discovered that when students from grade two and grade six are in the same classroom, both age groups perform better. In this setting, it is possible for all students to work at their appropriate skill levels and learn more effectively as a result. The grade six students are tutors and role models for grade two students, who now have friends and mentors in the older students. For parts of each day, students also work independently and with others their own age. Learning in this setting occurs for all students all day, every day, in a variety of ways.

Looping is another proven structure that allows teachers to work with the same group of children for more than 1 year. Teachers who are able to work with the same students over a period of years are in a much improved position to support the learning of their students. Relationships are established and ongoing, as is the teacher's understanding of each child as a learner. The transition from one year of learning to the next is seamless.

The staff at Monticello High School devised a number of strategies for addressing learning needs in flexible ways. Two of them are particularly noteworthy. The implementation of their 2-day rotating timetable allows for a full 60-minute period every other day during which students can be grouped according to learning needs to receive any extra time and support they require. Students at Monticello are arranged in cohorts, and, because teachers work in interdisciplinary team settings, they regularly share knowledge and observations about the students they have in common. As a result, they get to know their students well and can intervene early when difficulties surface. The fact that time for intervention is built right into the timetable every 2 days makes timely support possible.

The teacher mentorship program is another way that the Monticello staff has found to track and support students. All teachers mentor a group consisting of students from grades 9 through 12 who are not assigned to the classes they teach. The teachers and students get to know each other well over the 4-year period they have together. Early identification and individualized intervention are positive outcomes of this practice. The multi-age nature of the mentorship groups encourages students to support each other as well. The flexibility inherent in the unique timetable and the teacher mentorship program at Monticello can help address the learning needs of all students.

Professional learning communities provide a forum in which teachers can explore and develop flexible structures to meet student needs.

From planning to plan to planning to improve. In our work, we have seen that most schools have a plan; however, very few actually have a plan to improve. Often schools confuse planning to improve with choosing a new program or new textbook. Plans to improve focus on having an impact on student learning—whether the impact is felt in a specific discipline or in a social sense. Plans to improve are developed on a foundation of shared values and are based on the study of critical evidence. To have a positive overall impact on student achievement, clear goals are set which state the results to be achieved and lay out strategies for achieving them. Once implemented, plans need to be monitored on an ongoing basis to ascertain if they are, in fact, accomplishing what they were intended to accomplish.

From staff and time as fixed variables to learning as the fixed variable. In the traditional context, schools assume that staff size and qualifications as well as the timetable are fixed variables and that learning is the dependent variable. In other words, it is assumed that student learning is dependent on the number of teachers and class size and that the only way to improve student outcomes is to put more money toward education. We question this assumption. Would giving teachers a $1,000 bonus cause them to teach $1,000 harder? Would removing one student from each class result in increased student learning? Would 10 minutes added to math time mean that students would learn more math? We believe that the answer to all of these questions is "Maybe."

We assert that learning should be considered the fixed variable, and that all students can be supported to learn by flexing staff and time to meet their needs. Sacred Heart modified the school day to meet student needs. They started later and finished earlier to prevent fights with students from a neighboring school. They eliminated recess and added structured activities to allow all students to be part of a team and to prevent playground problems that would later influence classroom learning. They shortened the lunch period and introduced intervention and differentiated learning activities to address student needs. The roles and responsibilities of their resource staff were revised and unique classroom combinations were introduced. They established the Quiet Room and adjusted their staff allocation to guarantee the presence of a teacher in it at all times. At Sacred Heart, learning is fixed (not optional). Time and staff, traditionally considered the fixed variables, are flexible in this successful Harbor of Hope so that student needs can be addressed.

When teachers work in professional learning communities, the opportunities for increased flexibility are multiplied. There are times, for example, when one teacher can manage a large group of students in a planned activity while other staff members work with smaller groups. Two teachers working together can accommodate students by regrouping them for various components of the educational program. The options created by viewing time and deployment of staff as flexible are much greater when teachers work collaboratively in teams.

From learning for most to learning for all. "Learning for All—Whatever It Takes" requires that schools adjust to accommodate the needs of all students. Struggling students represent a challenge for teachers who may not know how to deal with them. Their personal competency needs may be threatened by these students. Many schools attempt to change these students so that they will fit the system by implementing special segregated programs, remedial programs, or referrals to programs outside of the school or district. Retention is also used for students who have academic lags. The premise behind these practices is that they will "fix up" the students involved so that they will be able to return to the mainstream and keep up with everyone else. If, however, students do not respond, the assumption is that they are unable and that they cannot be accommodated in the mainstream.

These approaches to students who are struggling can no longer be supported. So much is now known about differing learning styles and aptitudes, as well as differentiated instructional strategies, that it is imperative that we revisit past assumptions and practices pertaining to students who struggle. The reality is that once one layer of struggling students is removed to a special program, another layer of struggling students will surface. There is not enough time, money, or staff to continue to work this way. Finding special programs or services will not ensure that these students will learn; however, finding the appropriate instructional approach for them will.

At Monticello an entire program level was dropped and the staff discovered that, with support, most students were able to meet the increased expectations. Simply changing the levels did not accomplish the transformation. The staff had to work together to make it successful. An interdisciplinary approach to instruction, along with a focus on tracking student achievement through formative assessment, end-of-course assessments, and study of the Standards of Learning results helped to direct their efforts. Staff members formed interdisciplinary PLCs to work with cohorts of students. In that way it was possible to maintain a clear focus on the needs of the students and, hence, to be able to look for ways to ensure learning for all.

Summary

The reflection phase of the Planning for School and Student Success Process is where planning really begins. The critical evidence collected during the study phase is the stimulus for an analytical exploration of the current state of learning in a school. As the staff reflects on the critical evidence, it usually becomes evident that they should be working with others who share interests similar to their own. Professional learning communities provide the vehicle for teacher collaboration, which then leads to change and improved learning outcomes for all students. The journey toward hope is well under way.

Chapter 8

Plan

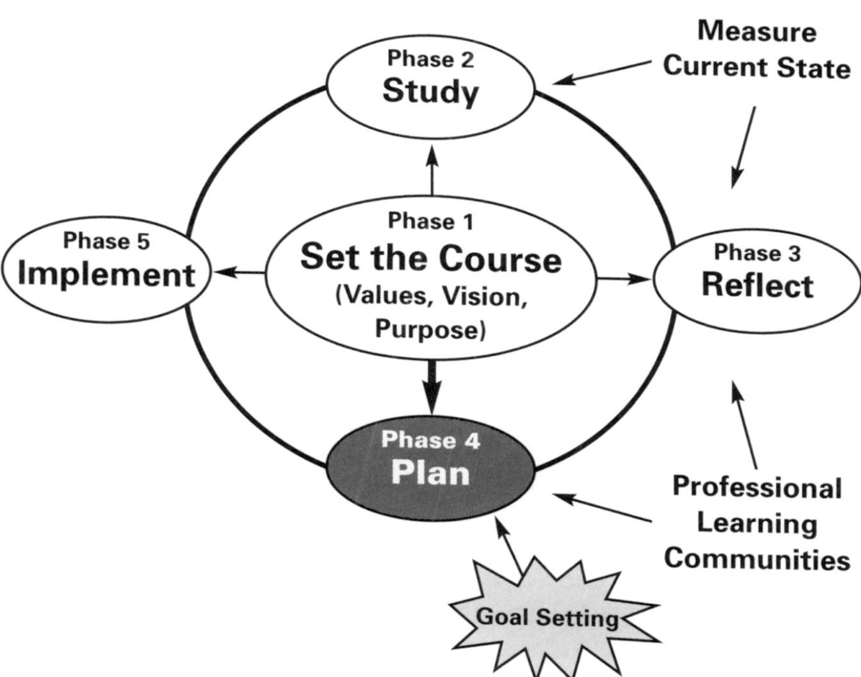

The Complexity of Reculturing

In the Planning for School and Student Success Process, reculturing is the aim. Reculturing is not simple because it involves so many people working collaboratively. Collaboration, the key activity, is good even when it occurs spontaneously in a school setting. But within the Planning for School and Student Success Process, collaboration is also a planned activity, and during the planning phase in particular, professional learning communities are the vehicles for change.

Teams and collaborative working relationships are not new to education. Open plan schools of the 1970s and 1980s were constructed to provide opportunities for teachers to work together by providing flexible structures. The concept of team teaching has been part of educational vocabulary for 50 years. Terrence Deal (1985) highlighted the importance of collaboration in the development of a positive school culture. When Fred Newmann (1998) looked at successful secondary schools, he found that success was based on "team collaboration among staff, sustained time for planning and curricula development, authority to act without unreasonable constraints and access to external assistance such as professional networks and organizations" (p. 95).

As much as the benefits of collaboration have been touted over the years, school cultures have not traditionally been supportive of actual efforts to collaborate. Roland Barth (1991) puts it this way: "God didn't create self-contained classrooms, fifty minute periods, and subjects taught in isolation. We did—because we find working alone safer than and preferable to working together" (p. 128). Teachers have tended to resist changes that may cause them to sense a loss of control. They are expected to control their students, and many feel they can best do this by having an individually assigned class in an individually assigned space. They are accustomed to a setup in which supervision and evaluation are based on their performance as individuals responsible for a designated group of students.

Teachers regularly get feedback that suggests that quiet classrooms are perceived as places where learning is occurring, whereas classrooms where children are moving about and talking to each other are considered to be disorderly, unproductive learning environments. Parents, based on their own school experiences, tend to expect quiet classrooms where children work independently—at their desks—on the "basic skills."

The fact that schools and systems strive for uniformity adds to the complexity of the reculturing process. Governments pass laws intended to ensure that all schools are working in a prescribed manner. Policies and procedures are created at the district level. Supervision practices do not typically encourage change. This factory-model mindset worked effectively when schools were seen as sorting institutions that determined which students would qualify for higher levels of education and which would go directly to the world of work. This model, however, is out of date both in business and in schools.

In business, the need for reculturing has been addressed by restructuring large organizations into smaller work units, each with a specific purpose. This restructuring adds flexibility and allows corporations to respond more quickly to the changing global economy. Schools can benefit from similar restructuring. Today's reality in schools is that the world has changed so substantially that it is no longer feasible for teachers to respond individually to the many demands they face in their work. The only solution is for them to collaborate with each other in order to address the many new curricula and varied student needs. Professional learning communities represent a powerful opportunity for this necessary collaboration. There are, however, some challenges to be addressed in the process.

The Challenges Facing Professional Learning Communities

When teachers begin to work collaboratively in professional learning settings, they soon realize that change is difficult. Some members may resist and interfere with the work of the team, others may feel overwhelmed, and still others may forge ahead too quickly. As they learn to work together, members of the PLC may experience the lure of doing business the "old way." Three common challenges faced by professional learning communities in their work are:

- Procrastination: *planning to plan* rather than *planning to improve*
- Resistance: clinging to the status quo
- Over-reaching: trying to do too much too soon

Procrastination. A professional learning community can easily fall into the trap of *planning to plan* rather than *planning to improve.* It is not uncommon for schools to decide to implement innovative programs as part of their school plan. When this happens, we may see initiatives like the following:

- Implement whole-language instruction in every classroom.
- Introduce cooperative learning.
- Create professional learning communities.
- Introduce a safe school policy.
- Redesign the progress report to reflect more authentic assessment of student performance.
- Have each teacher implement three new teaching strategies before the Christmas break.

- Integrate technology into the curriculum.

Carl Glickman (1993) contends that the "litmus test for a good school is not its innovations but rather the solid, purposeful, enduring results it obtains for its students" (p. 50). Stephen Covey (1989) tells us that "an effective goal focuses primarily on results rather than on activity. It identifies where you want to be . . . gives you important information on how to get there, and it tells you when you have arrived. It unifies your efforts and energy" (p. 137). Mike Schmoker (2001) captures the difference between planning to plan and planning to improve in this explanation:

> Establishing vague process or procedural goals in the absence of clear, concrete learning goals is foolish. Each undergirds the other. Learning goals give meaning to and act as a healthy check on the traditionally unfettered tendency for public institutions to be satisfied with processes, regardless of outcomes. (p. 30)

Resistance. School improvement is hard work. It is messy as well, in the sense that requirements for change are seldom straightforward, nor are they often enthusiastically embraced. While some teachers will embrace immediately the opportunity to work with their colleagues, others may resent the expectation that they work differently. It is essential that teachers have agreed on shared values, vision, and purpose—these form the foundation for all conversations. Other supports in terms of professional development, time for collaboration, materials to support instruction, and general encouragement will also be required to facilitate the process.

DuFour and Eaker (1998) tell us that "collaboration by invitation does not work" (p. 118). If teachers are to collaborate effectively, they must have time for reflection, collective inquiry, planning, and professional support. Teams must be given specific direction regarding activities to be completed as well as the training and support to work together effectively. As teachers gain expertise and confidence in their roles as members of a team, collaboration and peer support will become embedded in the culture of the school.

Prerequisites for Creating Effective Collaborative Teams
(Adapted from DuFour and Eaker, 1998)

1. Time must be established specifically for collaboration.
2. The purpose of collaboration must be made explicit.
3. School personnel need training and support if they are to be effective collaborators.
4. Educators must accept their professional responsibility to work with their colleagues.

Over-reaching. There is a risk of attempting to do too much too soon with the result that people feel overwhelmed, exhausted, and discouraged—responses that do not bode well for enduring change. Clearly, it is not possible to do everything all at once, so where should the planning process begin? What is the best use of staff time and energy? Which goals ought to be priorities for now, and which should be deferred for later? The

number and nature of goals that are set in the planning phase are critical to the success of the process.

In order to avoid overload, it is important that each professional learning community identify no more than three goals to work on. The goals of all of the PLCs will ultimately form the overall school improvement plan. The school plan may have many goals, but the involvement of individual staff members will be limited to no more than three goals.

Setting Goals (Beyond Percentages and Numbers)

The planning phase of the Planning for School and Student Success Process focuses on setting goals that will make a difference in the lives of students and inspire staff commitment to achieving better results. Many planning models focus primarily on improving academic outcomes at specific levels, in specific disciplines, for specific groups of students. We, too, are committed to improving academic outcomes for all students, and we believe that these goals are very important. We believe, however, that to create schools that are true Harbors of Hope, attention must also be given to equally important goals that go beyond academic achievement.

Stephen Covey (1989) points out that personal effectiveness results from a combination of character and competence traits. When people behave in ways that display both character and competence, they come to be seen as trustworthy. Covey's thinking applies equally well to the school setting. Schools that are worthy of the trust of students and their communities must also display character and competence. They must also be seen as trustworthy.

Highly effective schools set both character and competence goals. Character goals are usually school-wide and have an impact on the culture of the school. Competence goals tend to be academic and are student- or discipline-specific. Both character and competence goals focus on learning and improved student outcomes. What makes them distinct from each other is their focus.

Much of the current writing about school improvement centers on what we call the competence goals. These goals tend to have a narrow focus with an emphasis on measuring improvement using numbers and percentages. Our concern is that when schools focus only on academic achievement, the heart and passion that reside in school-wide character goals will go untapped. School-wide goals pertain to things such as student leadership, ritual and celebration, teamwork, social responsibility, the arts, health and fitness, parent involvement, multiculturalism, and anti-bullying. These are the areas that we consider the "umbrella curriculum," because of their protective reach. We believe that skill and knowledge in these areas are as important to the development of the whole child as are the skills of literacy and numeracy. They involve life-skills learning and have a notable impact on the development of each student as well as on the character of the school. Goals for learning in these areas enhance school culture by providing opportunities for all students to excel. They also assist in creating the sense of community needed by students if they are to experience feelings of belonging and support as they learn and develop as individuals. School-wide character goals combine with academic, discipline-specific competence goals to create Harbors of Hope. The combination is powerful.

All three of the schools that have been presented in this book as Harbors of Hope have based their planning on both character and competence goals. In all cases, their commitment to both originated with their statements of values, vision, and purpose. Without exception, our Harbors of Hope worked at improving school culture through focusing on the development of the whole child with specific emphasis on skill development in academic areas.

Character, Competence, and the Correlates of Effective Schools

We believe that the correlates of effective schools, identified by Lawrence Lezotte, illustrate the relationship between character and competence in schools that are worthy of the trust of students and the community. Instructional leadership has an impact on both the character and competence correlates.

Character Correlates	Competence Correlates
• Shared common purpose (clear and focused mission)	• Opportunity to learn and time on task
• Safe and orderly environment	• Climate of high expectations for success
• Positive home-school relations	• Frequent monitoring of student progress

• Instructional leadership

Character Correlates

Shared common purpose (clear and focused mission). Effective schools have clearly stated values, vision, and purpose that are understood and accepted by staff. When staff members commit to things like learning for all, wellness, social responsibility, or community service, they set character goals to be achieved by all students in the school. These school-wide goals may be realized in different ways with students of different ages and abilities. They will be a focus for all staff in all respects of the life of the school.

Safe and orderly environment. When staff members set a goal to reduce bullying or to introduce social responsibility, they are working to affect the culture of the school by creating an environment that will positively support and influence all aspects of learning.

Positive home-school relations. Improved communication with parents and their meaningful involvement in supporting the learning of their children are powerful ways to improve student outcomes.

Competence Correlates

Opportunity to learn and time on task. When specific learning outcomes for specific groups of students in specific disciplines are established, building competence in those areas becomes the focus. It is important to look at both instructional strategies and the use of time when focusing on increasing student achievement. Learning activities that fully engage students will increase time on task. Time on task is also increased when the timetable and school structures are established to maximize learning activity. Students experience success when they are

exposed to inspiring learning opportunities in flexible classroom groupings. The structure of learning activities, grouping practices, and interventions for struggling students, along with the use of unstructured time and the question of homework, are all important considerations in this regard.

Climate of high expectations for success. Setting competency goals or standards to be reached is one way of conveying high expectations. Persistence in providing time and instruction for students until they succeed is another. Teacher/student/parent interactions are the arena for communicating high expectations for success and for providing the support students require to meet them. The culture of the school can communicate high expectations by recognizing and celebrating the accomplishments of all students as they learn and grow.

Frequent monitoring of student progress. Teacher competency in monitoring and assessing student progress is essential to school and student improvement. Assessment directs teaching, supports planning, and provides the means for evaluating the effectiveness of instruction. Rubrics, along with varied forms of authentic assessment, are valuable tools for helping students become aware of themselves as learners. As students begin to understand their unique characteristics as learners, and as they "learn how to learn," they are acquiring competencies they need for their futures. When teachers prepare students for local or government tests, they focus on the curricular outcomes identified as essential or standard and, at the same time, develop test-taking skills so that students can show what they know.

The Seventh Correlate: Instructional Leadership

The instructional leadership correlate is integral to the development of both the character and competence correlates. The character of a school is positive when its culture supports the empowerment and reasonable risk taking that results in teachers becoming instructional leaders. Leadership is about influence. Working in an environment of safety and order, with parents or caregivers as partners, staff members can support students in taking the risks that are required to learn. In this environment, the staff is guided by a shared, common purpose as they collaborate to meet student needs and to "invent work worth doing." These proactive professional attitudes create a culture of trust and respect that positively affects the school's character.

Instructional leadership also has an impact on the competence of students and staff. Everyone in the school community is viewed as a learner. Teachers, working together, focus on the conditions for learning that will result in greater skill, knowledge, and abilities for their students and for themselves. Critical evidence is gathered to measure the success of students' efforts, and high-yield strategies are implemented to enhance learning outcomes for all. Students are assured of the opportunity to learn with sufficient time on task in a climate of high expectations where their progress is frequently monitored. As a result, both teacher and student competence is positively affected.

Setting Goals That Will Make a Difference

Lezotte and McKee (2002) refer to effective goal statements as "improvement objectives" that will be clear to anyone who reads them. Improvement objectives answer the following questions:

- Who will perform?
- What activity will be performed?
- When will it be performed?
- How will it be measured?

An improvement objective might read:

> By the last week of June, at least 80 percent of the girls in grades 2 to 5 will have mastered the essential mathematics learning for their grade level. The evidence used will be end-of-year grades of C or higher in grades 2 to 5, as well as a score of proficient on the mathematics portion of the state standardized test for fourth graders. (p. 176)

Anne Conzemius and Jan O'Neill (2002) teach us about SMART goals. They believe that "because SMART goals provide a basis for assessing progress, and a tool for assuring that team efforts are focused on strategically important targets, they become the engine that drives continuous improvement and learning" (p. 6). SMART goals are **S**trategic and **S**pecific, **M**easurable, **A**ttainable, **R**esults-based, and **T**ime-bound.

An example of a SMART goal would be the following:

> Within the next 3 years, 100% of all third-grade students will achieve the proficiency level in reading and mathematics.

This goal is specific, measurable, attainable, results-based, and time-bound. Attainment of this goal is possible only if all teachers from kindergarten to third grade share it and work together to achieve it. Examination of the critical evidence gathered in phase 2—the study phase—of the planning process will provide baseline information about the present achievement of third-grade students. This information will help teachers decide where to begin with instruction. It is also useful in tracking the impact of instruction over time.

SMART Goals Are . . .

- **S**trategic and specific—goals will be based on the critical evidence and focused on specific student learning needs.
- **M**easurable—progress and success will be measured in numerous ways, using a variety of tools and methods.
- **A**ttainable—the challenge of achieving the goal must be balanced with the time and resources that are available.
- **R**esults-based—specific learning outcomes will be identified, as well as how they will be measured or observed.
- **T**ime-bound—reasonable and attainable timelines will add urgency to the goal and keep it a priority.

Summary

Teachers working collaboratively in professional learning communities are the key to successful school improvement. They will face challenges as they work to set goals and develop plans for achieving them. Careful goal setting intended to address both character and competence is essential to effective planning. School-wide goals are most apt to focus on character development and school culture, whereas student- or discipline-specific goals will focus on the development of competence.

Goals must be carefully crafted to focus planning and implementation. Well-thought-out goals will be based on consideration of both qualitative and quantitative critical evidence. They will reflect the values that have been identified by the school community. Zmuda and associates (2004) refer to improving schools as competent systems that serve the end of enhanced achievement for all students. They tell us that in a competent system, "all staff members believe that what they have collectively agreed to do is challenging, possible and worthy of the attempt" (p. 183).

Chapter 9

High-Yield Strategies: Keys to Goal Attainment

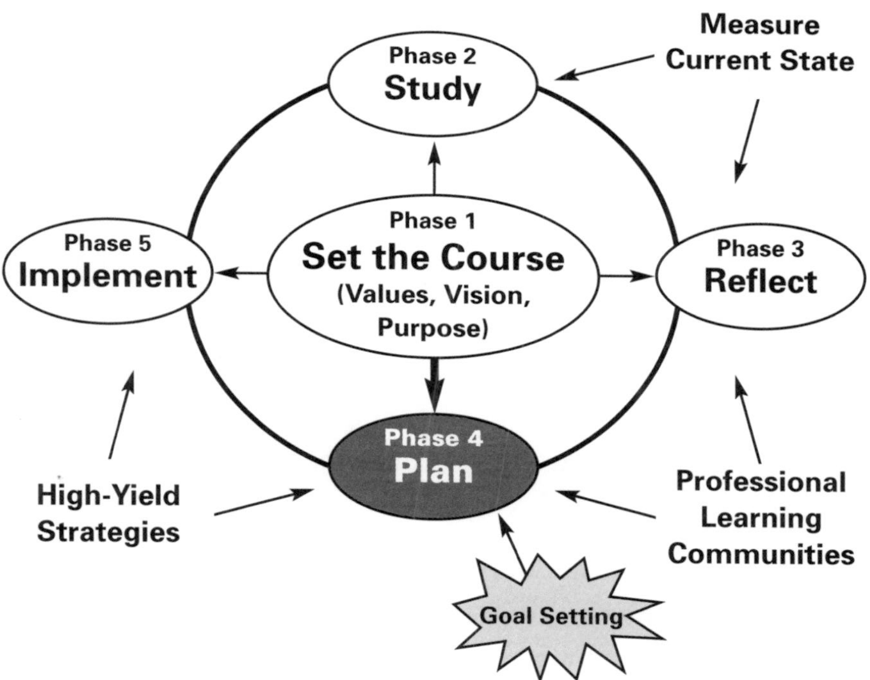

When professional learning communities plan for school and student success, they reflect on critical evidence in order to set goals for school improvement. Once goals have been set, staff members engage in the planning phase of the process by asking critical questions to guide their planning (see below) and by identifying high-yield strategies that will help the school staff meet their goals. High-yield strategies exist for both character and competence goals.

Critical Questions to Guide Planning

1. What do our students need to learn if they are to succeed?
2. What are we going to do to ensure they learn it?
3. How will we measure to ensure they are learning it?
4. What will we do when they are not learning what they need to learn to succeed?

Lezotte (1997) defines a high-yield strategy as "a concept or principle, supported by research or case literature that will, when successfully applied in a real school setting, result in significant improvement in assessed student achievement" (p. 17). He contends that high-yield strategies change the transaction and interaction between the teacher and students or among students.

Building a new school roof is a strategy for keeping teachers and students dry, but it will not significantly increase achievement. Cooperative learning, however, if properly implemented, will change the relationship between students and teachers and can have an enormous impact on student success in the classroom and on the playground. It is important to track student outcomes as we implement high-yield strategies in

order to be assured that these strategies are, in fact, resulting in improvement.

Staff development, research, and focused collaboration are keys to identifying the high-yield strategies that will be most effective at improving school and student outcomes in terms of goals that have been set.

Four Focus Areas for High-Yield Strategies

1. School structures and practices
2. Curriculum alignment
3. Instructional practices
4. Parent involvement

This chapter describes four focus areas for high-yield strategies that Harbors of Hope can draw upon to achieve goals.

Area One: School Structures and Practices

School structures and practices should be reviewed to determine those that best support student learning and those that may interfere with learning. School structures include the physical setup of the school, staff allocation and assignment, and student groupings and timetables. School practices include reporting processes, student recognition systems, behavior management, support and intervention for struggling students, codes of conduct, homework, and attendance policies.

Charlotte Danielson (2002) speaks of the aspects of a school's organizational structure as being "highly intertwined and tightly related to other aspects of the school, such as curriculum, student assessment, and learning support" (p. 47). It is very important that we review existing structures and practices with an open mind and the flexibility to make changes to support optimal learning opportunities for all students in an atmosphere of safety and respect.

We have created the following 10-point audit to help schools assess the effectiveness of their structures and practices. The critical evidence that will provide direction in these areas will come from students, staff, parents, and the community.

1. Is our school environment safe and orderly?
2. Are we deploying our staff to maximize learning?
3. Are we grouping students to maximize learning?
4. Are we effectively supporting students who are struggling?
5. Does our timetable support the learning process?
6. Are our reporting practices adequate and effective?
7. Are our student recognition practices respectful and encouraging?
8. Is the philosophy behind our discipline policy understood by all?
9. Is the philosophy behind our homework policy and practice understood by all?
10. Does our attendance policy support student learning?

1. Is our school environment safe and orderly? A well-thought-out plan for the use of school space and time can go a long way toward helping students of all ages to feel secure at school. Students need to feel physically safe at school during both structured and unstructured times. Are they comfortable

in the locker room? Do older students think of themselves as friends and mentors to younger students? Are the youngest members in the school community welcomed without any intimidating initiation rites? Do students know that the adults in the school will protect and ensure their physical and emotional safety? Is the school's position on bullying and other safety issues clearly articulated and communicated?

Belonging to and being a valued member of a community are prerequisites for a solid learning environment. The adults in a school have a major role to play in this regard. Visible presence in hallways, cafeterias, locker rooms, and playgrounds allows adults in the school to monitor and support students during unstructured times. Keeping students in class cohorts as much as possible is a method of building community. Teacher-advisor and house systems—both ways of ensuring unthreatening adult sponsorship—are two other methods that may be useful in certain school environments. Emotional and physical safety of students can be more easily assured if there are systems in place that connect them to at least one caring adult in the school. Every student should know that there is an adult at the school who cares if the student has a problem and will notice if he or she is ill or absent. Physical safety and freedom from harassment are essential conditions for learning.

All adults in the school have an important role to play in creating a culture that is supportive of student learning. Not just teachers, but also clerical staff, custodians, bus drivers, and cafeteria/lunch supervisors should participate in the process of articulating values, vision, and purpose statements, or should, at the very least, understand them clearly. It is also important to include them with classroom teachers in professional development pertaining to classroom and behavior management. The student's day does not usually begin in the classroom; it begins en route to school and in the activities leading up to the first class, whether those activities occur in a breakfast program, on the playground, in the hallways, or in extracurricular activities. Douglas Reeves (2004) speaks of the value of leaders taking steps to achieve consistency in the education and behavior of all adults in the school and in so doing ensuring that "every staff member, from the bus driver to the food service employee to the classroom teacher, is regarded as a significant adult leader in the eyes of students" (p. 72). When adults are consistent in language and interactions, student behavior is positively affected and the stage is set for productive learning and achievement.

2. Are we deploying our staff to maximize learning? School staff is generally allocated according to a district formula based on perceived needs for "regular" instruction and "specialist" instruction in areas such as music, physical education, visual arts, ESL, special education/gifted education, technology, and so on. Explicit and deliberate involvement of all teachers in curriculum implementation, regardless of their role in the school, leads to improved outcomes for all students. Reeves (2004) cites the example of examination of critical evidence in mathematics that has revealed unsatisfactory scores in the skills pertaining to fractions, ratios, and measurement. He maintains that although these are skills identified in the mathematics curriculum, involving other disciplines in the instruction will teach and reinforce the skills in a variety of ways. For instance, music teachers can help by focusing on rhythmic notation and the mathematical relationships between notes. Physical education teachers can use running to illustrate fractions, ratios, and measurement. Art teachers can incorporate math into their instruction when they discuss and demonstrate perspective and scale. Other disciplines can be integrated as well. Social studies units lend themselves particularly well to integration with language arts, mathematics, music, visual arts, and physical education activities. There is an obvious role for special education, gifted education, and technology teachers in all curricula. Horizontal mapping for curriculum integration permits teachers in all disciplines to maximize instructional time.

3. Are we grouping students to maximize learning? Research suggests that class sizes of 15 or fewer will maximize learning opportunities for students. In the "real world," it is not likely that we will ever have classes of this size. What we can understand, however, is that smaller instructional groups are likely to result in improved learning. The goal is to determine how to utilize the staff in ways that will create smaller instructional groups for part of each day.

Student grouping is a philosophical issue that needs to be addressed at the staff level in response to questions such as the following:

- How do we make decisions about student class placement? By ability, personality?
- Do we subscribe to homogeneous groupings or do we support the notion of heterogeneous groupings?
- How do we group students within the classroom? Are in-class groupings flexible or static? Do we use group names like "bluebirds" and "buzzards" which may, in subtle (or not so subtle) ways, indicate achievement levels?

The answers to these questions will reveal the philosophy about student grouping in a school.

Our endorsement of smaller instructional groups is also a vote against old-fashioned tracking. We strongly support what Danielson (2002) tells us about grouping strategies and could not have said it any more succinctly than she does:

> Permanent tracking harms all but the highest-performing students, who themselves gain only slightly from the practice. Short-term skill grouping, however, can be highly beneficial for all students. . . . The school's approach to scheduling and deployment of staff must support the formation of short-term skill groups when needed. In addition, the school's organization must allow for skill groups to be formed quickly and changed frequently; flexibility, in other words, is the key. (p. 47)

4. Are we effectively supporting students who are struggling? Student support services are central to the functioning of any school. There are many different models and philosophies for service delivery in this area. A staff's stated values, vision, and purpose will guide their work with students who experience difficulty.

As schools reflect on their structures and practices for supporting struggling students, they must explore the answers to a number of questions:

- Are we committed to inclusion for all of our students?
- What do we mean when we say we are inclusive?
- Do student support services exist for all students in our school or just for some? Are we providing the right kind of support?
- Are we using assessment information to determine the learning styles and needs of struggling students?

- Are we providing assistance to appropriately plan instruction for those students?
- How are we supporting these students as they learn?
- Are we including parents/caregivers as partners in our work with these students?

Schmoker (2002) reports on the work of Rick DuFour and his staff at Adlai Stevenson High School. The "pyramid of interventions" at Stevenson was developed to provide support to students if they experienced difficulty. The "pyramid" is essentially a continuum of gradually intensified interventions to be followed with students who are not achieving. Teachers at Stevenson are responsible for monitoring the achievement of their students and intervening at the first sign of difficulty. Interventions range from gentle reminders through extensive planning for support involving additional staff and intervention beyond the classroom.

In our work with teachers, we have encouraged them to think of intervention strategies in three contexts: the classroom, the school, and the broader community, where the classroom or subject teacher is the key to the entire process. We advocate that the process begin with the development of a profile for each student that includes pertinent information about a variety of things, such as current skill levels, past achievement, attendance, attitudes, and behaviors. This information provides guidance for teachers as they plan learning experiences, instructional strategies, and supports. Additional classroom resources exist and can be employed to assist the work of students as they learn. If more assistance is required than what can be accommodated in the classroom, school-based resources can be accessed and, if necessary, supports within the broader community can be employed. The following diagram illustrates our strategy.

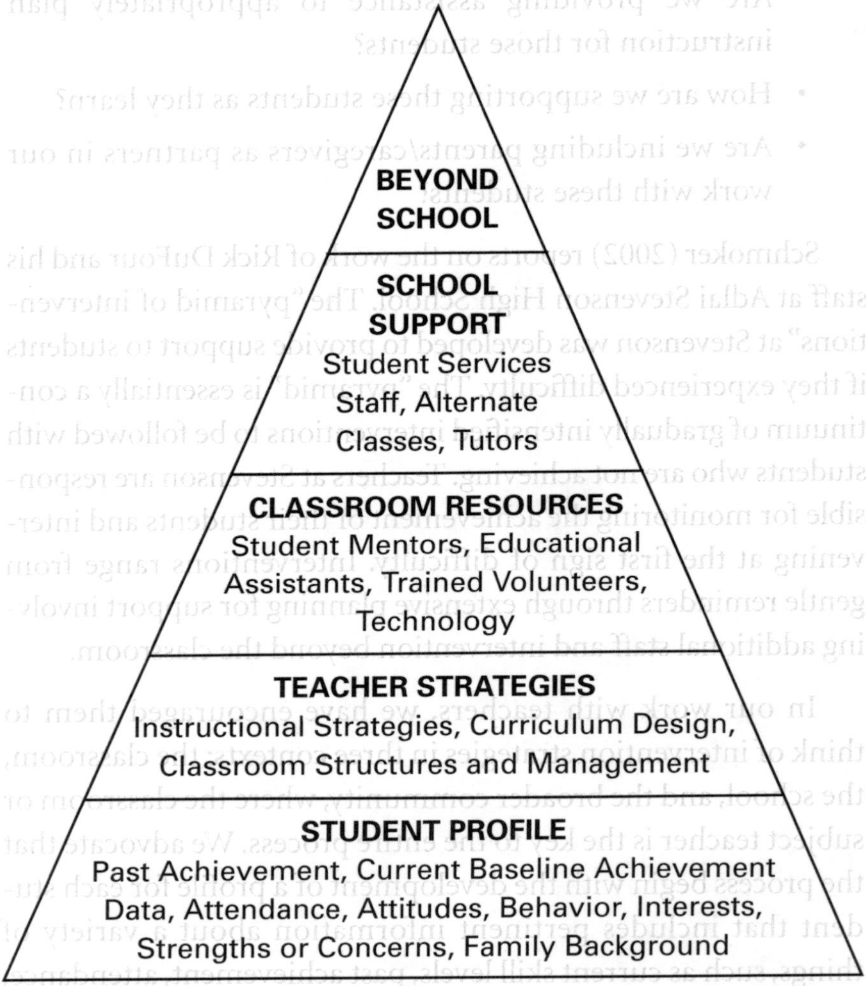

—Adapted from DuFour, DuFour, Eaker, and Karhanek (2004)

This kind of approach was taken by the staff of Sacred Heart Community School when they completely revamped their student support service structure to focus on the use of high-yield instructional strategies to support larger numbers of students. Direct support to the classroom became a primary concern for those teachers working in student support services. The staff at

Lawrence Heights Middle School developed numerous programs to support struggling students. The Project Pride and B.A.S.E. programs were two of them. Monticello High School has been diligent in its commitment to providing extra time and instruction for those who struggle by altering the school's schedule to build in time for intervention.

5. Does our timetable support the learning process? Reeves (2004) has noted that "the essential importance of instructional time is hardly a new idea, yet in an astonishing number of schools, the schedule is revered more than the Pledge of Allegiance, the Constitution, and the Magna Carta combined" (p. 68). Class length, the time of day in which various subjects are taught, and the availability of common teacher preparation times are some of the things that are dictated by the timetable. It is important to consider the pace of the day and whether students derive maximum benefit from the timetable that is in place. The following questions will help staff members address this issue:

- Would double class length be more effective?
- Which parts of the day are prime learning times and how should we be using them?
- Which skills need daily practice? Which ones can be acquired through exposure at regular intervals?
- Are we maximizing the "zero hour" options such as before and after school times as well as the lunch hour?
- Does the timetable allow for flexible groupings? When will the professional learning communities work together?

Most schools that are committed to increasing student achievement have thrown out the traditional timetable models in favor of doing what is required to maximize opportunities to learn. Some schools are substantially increasing the amount of instructional time devoted to literacy and numeracy by decreasing the time allocated to other subject areas. We contend that this measure is harsh and unnecessary. In our opinion, it is possible to enhance skill levels in literacy and numeracy without sacrificing learning in the other areas that are so important for the development of well-rounded students. Curriculum mapping that is both horizontal (between grades) and lateral (between disciplines) identifies essential learning outcomes, illustrates instructional integration possibilities, and provides a curricular "road map" for teachers to follow as they assess their students and plan for instruction.

There are many ways to be creative in the construction of a school's timetable. Before that happens, however, the staff must identify what they believe about curricular priorities and the learning conditions that are desirable for both students and teachers.

6. Are our reporting practices adequate and effective? When we report on student progress, we are simply taking a snapshot of how that student is achieving at a moment in time. Reporting practices typically take the form of conferences, along with interim progress reports and end-of-term report cards. Our goal in reporting should be twofold: (1) to communicate student progress to the student, to parents, and to other teachers and (2) to support students in setting goals to overcome difficulties and improve for the next reporting period. Consider the following questions:

- Are we communicating effectively through our reporting process?

- Is the communication timely?
- Are we effectively involving parents in the process?
- Is the goal-setting process effective?
- Do our reporting practices reflect curriculum outcomes?
- Are we giving a complete picture of each student's school experience?
- Are we providing necessary feedback to students between reporting periods?

Reeves (2004) found that "schools with significant improvements provided much more frequent feedback to students than a report card typically provides" (p. 67).

7. Are our student recognition practices respectful and encouraging? Student learning is not limited to formal learning activities related to the curriculum. It occurs through extra- and co-curricular involvement as well as incidentally through day-to-day occurrences in the school. Recognition of student growth and achievement should be an integral part of the school culture and should not be limited to high academic scores or honors won through athletic or fine arts accomplishments. Students who work hard to improve are every bit as worthy as those who earn top grades. Those who write poetry or create the program for the school musical should also be recognized and celebrated.

Goleman (1998) contends that emotional intelligence (EQ) has a much greater impact than intelligence quotient (IQ) on success in the workplace. Students' ability to communicate, solve problems, and work collaboratively in teams is critical to their long-term success. These competencies ought to be as routinely recognized as academic skills.

A culture of student recognition is illustrated through such things as displays of student work, celebration assemblies, honor rolls, student-of-the-week projects, and lunch with the principal. Of course, the nature of student recognition practices must change to remain age-appropriate as students progress through school. The importance of student recognition, however, never goes away.

8. Is the philosophy behind our discipline policy understood by all? Rather than using the term "discipline policy," we prefer to think in terms of a "code of conduct" which outlines behavioral guidelines and responsibilities for all members of the community: students, staff, and parents. Ideally, the philosophy informing a code of conduct would see "discipline" as a learning opportunity for students. In such an approach, parents and teachers are seen as models, mentors, and coaches for students. The importance of their partnership in support of students is stated in a code of conduct which clearly articulates lines of communication and processes for responding to behavioral issues. The important questions about a code of conduct are:

- Is it respectful to all people?
- Is the philosophy clearly stated?
- Are the "bottom lines" pertaining to extreme behavior identified and communicated?

Clear and thoughtful practices relating to behavior management, discipline, and personal conduct have a major impact on the culture of a school. They should not be punitive or founded in a hierarchy of power; instead, they should set the stage for student learning and respectful relationships in a climate that is safe for all.

9. Is the philosophy behind our homework policy and practice understood by all? A well-designed homework policy helps students organize themselves, take responsibility for their learning, and extend that learning beyond the school day. An effective homework policy would incorporate the following guidelines:

- Homework should be meaningful work that is related to curricular outcomes. If it is important enough to be assigned, it should be important enough for all students to complete it.
- Student age should guide the kind of homework assigned. It is unreasonable to give younger children long hours of homework, though it is reasonable to expect them to do regular reading or mathematics practice at home. Teachers can encourage parents of younger children to support their children's learning by doing things such as reading, mapping-out trips, and comparing prices at the grocery store.
- Homework should provide practice for students as they consolidate their learning in new areas. Students should be able to complete this kind of homework independently. It is important to ensure that they have a grasp on the material before they attempt to do homework on it so that they are not practicing mistakes.
- A student's grades should reflect student mastery of material, not their consistency of homework completion. If a student is unable to finish homework, it is important to find out why. Was there an unexpected interruption at home that interfered? Was the student genuinely "stuck" and unable to complete the work? Regardless of the reason

homework may be incomplete, an alternate plan should be developed to get the work finished. Reporting on homework completion is appropriately placed under the heading of "work habits." It should not be reflected in or negatively affect the grade for that subject.

- Major assignments should be coordinated among teachers of different subjects so as to avoid student overload.

10. Does our attendance policy support student learning? An effective attendance policy maximizes time in school and recognizes that absences may be unavoidable at times. Individual circumstances are sometimes beyond a student's control and must be considered. Health issues or home challenges may interfere with attendance.

"Learning for All—Whatever It Takes" would indicate that commitment to getting and keeping students connected to the school is extremely important. Attendance is a powerful indicator of student success, along with attitude, behavior, and achievement. When attendance is an issue, it is probably time to take a close look at a student's achievement patterns in school. Keeping students connected to the school must be a priority because there is a danger that students may never return to school if they lose their connection to it. Individual tutoring or counseling may be required to help students stay connected to the school.

Danielson (2002) is strong in her position that the goal of school policies and practices should be student achievement of curricular outcomes along with support for their overall growth and development as individuals: "There is no room in a school truly committed to student learning for policies that are punitive, turn students away, or undermine their self-confidence" (p. 51). We certainly support this position.

Area Two: Curriculum Alignment

Three Curricula to Align

1. The *intended* curriculum
2. The *taught* curriculum
3. The *assessed* curriculum

Lezotte and McKee (2002) identify three curricula at each level in any given discipline: that which is intended, that which is taught, and that which is assessed. When there is poor alignment between the three, the result is student failure. When they are aligned, however, there is every opportunity for student success. According to Lezotte and McKee, state or provincial standards and stakeholder expectations come together "like two tributaries of a river merging into the intended curriculum":

> When there is poor curriculum alignment, the assessed curriculum ends up on one bank and the taught curriculum on the other and our students end up "missing the boat." When curriculum is properly aligned, we all end up "in the same boat" headed for student success! (p. 142)

Marzano (2003) speaks of a "guaranteed and viable curriculum" in which Opportunity to Learn (OTL) is a prominent factor in student success (p. 23). A guaranteed and viable curriculum specifies the content that teachers are expected to address in the time that is available to them. With the recent advent of so much new curricular material, time has become an enormous issue for teachers. Since there is simply not enough of it to allow adequate "coverage" of everything in the new curricula, the only solution is for educators to practice "selective abandonment." They must decide what not to teach and, in order to do so, they must develop a process for identifying essential learnings and eliminating non-essential material. DuFour and Eaker (1998) refer to this process as "addition by subtraction." "By subtracting content from the curriculum," they claim, "schools can strengthen their ability to help students master essential knowledge and skills" (p. 166).

Selective Abandonment—Who Decides?

Teachers, through collaboration, are in the best position to identify essential learnings and curricular goals. They are the trained professionals who, in the final analysis, will be responsible for helping students achieve the outcomes of the intended curriculum. When they engage in the key activity, collaboration, to develop the three curricula, their experience and training come into play. It is important that they have authority to make important decisions for which they are ultimately responsible. State or provincial standards along with those that have been determined locally are the foundation for this decision-making process.

Key Characteristics of the Curriculum Alignment Process

Begin with the end in mind. We borrow this admonition from Stephen Covey (1989), who identifies this as an important habit for highly effective people and organizations. Thinking about this habit within the context of curriculum alignment would result in a collaborative process of what Lezotte and McKee (2002) identify as "backward mapping" to identify the prerequisite knowledge and skills needed by students at each level that will prepare them for the next one. DuFour and Eaker (1998) speak of involving students, parents, and teachers in the identification of "specific knowledge, skills, and dispositions that students should acquire as a result of their schooling" (p. 157). Marzano (2003) takes a slightly different approach and speaks of "identifying and communicating the content considered essential for all students versus that considered supplemental or necessary only for those seeking postsecondary education" (p. 25).

The main goal here is to identify and sequence what students should know and be able to do. Sequencing ensures that students are able to progress through school achieving success at each step as a result of alignment between the intended, taught, and assessed curricula. When essential learnings are identified at each level, a continuum is established that makes the goal of continuous progress for individual students feasible.

Collaborate for alignment. Teacher involvement in the curriculum alignment process facilitates collective decisions about what students should know and be able to do. Such collaborative decisions provide guidance for teachers in their work with students. Marzano (2003) tells us that studies have shown that "teachers commonly make independent and idiosyncratic decisions regarding what should be covered and to what extent." (p. 23). This practice frequently results in large discrepancies between what is taught and what is assessed. As a result, achievement is adversely affected. He cautions that "if students do not have the opportunity to learn the content expected of them, there is little chance that they will" (p. 24). This insight seems so obvious that one wonders why it is so misunderstood.

Teachers working within the professional learning community context are in the best position to examine existing standards with a view to deciding which ones will be included as "essential learnings" in a given curriculum. The identification of essential learnings results in the articulation of the ***intended curriculum.*** Once this has been accomplished, performance indicators or benchmarks that define success can be developed, and learning experiences to help students reach those benchmarks can be chosen. Additionally, the material can be sequenced in order to give students adequate opportunity and time to meet the identified standards or absorb essential learnings. This sequencing results in the articulation of the ***taught curriculum.***

Appropriate and frequent assessment is imperative in ascertaining whether students are, in fact, achieving the benchmarks that have been set. Assessment that provides both formative and summative information is vital to teachers for determining the fit between *intended* and *taught* curricula. This information helps teachers adjust and refine their instructional strategies so that students are successful in the ***assessed curriculum.***

Heidi Hayes Jacobs (1997) introduced the curriculum mapping strategy to help with curriculum alignment. Curriculum mapping provides two different lenses, as Jacobs puts it, through which to look at a curriculum: "a zoom lens into this year's curriculum for a particular grade and a wide-angle lens to see the K-12 perspective" (p. 3). The value of these two perspectives is that they provide information about:

- Gaps and repetitions in content at the same grade level and across grade levels
- Areas of emphasis and gaps between the local curriculum and state or provincial standards

- Big ideas or concepts that are transferable over time (across grades, across subjects, in the "real world")
- The range of assessment vehicles used to evaluate student work

Curriculum maps provide powerful sources of information to be considered as teachers identify what students are expected to know and be able to do. The maps are also a valuable reference as teachers plan the sequencing of instruction that will allow them to bridge the various levels on the essential skills continuum.

It is true that working collectively to determine essential learnings and their benchmarks, along with instructional strategies and methods of assessment, requires teachers to give up some of their individual autonomy. The outcomes for students, however, are so significantly enhanced that the benefits far outweigh the drawbacks. If we recall what is shared in chapter 1 about the successful work performed by the staffs of Sacred Heart and Monticello, the benefits of this kind of collaboration are easily recognized. The challenge, of course, is to ensure that all teachers do, in fact, address the essential content, for it is only in this way that a viable curriculum that aligns intended, taught, and assessed content can be guaranteed.

Area Three: Instructional Practices

Everyone benefits when teachers collaborate to plan and implement curriculum. Students benefit from strategic instruction and teachers benefit from collegial interactions that enhance their competence as educators. The ultimate goal when teachers work together to plan instruction is that all students, at all levels, master the essential learnings. Working in this way prevents teachers from thinking of only certain students as their responsibility. Quality assessment practices, used in a collaborative setting, help teachers understand what students know before they engage in learning activities, as well as what they know as a result of their learning. There is no point in considering material "taught" if students have not learned it. Teachers working in teams have greater flexibility for grouping students and differentiating instruction. Planning for instruction will take into consideration the fact that meeting the needs of all students is complex work that requires in-depth understanding of both curriculum and the learning process. We conceive of four important "Connections for Instruction" that will assist in this work.

Connections for Instruction

- Basic skills/concept skills
- Strategy/style
- Teacher/student learning
- Instruction/assessment

Curriculum knowledge: The basic skills/concept skills connection. Danielson (2002) tells us that successful planning for instruction takes into account the fact that learning activities center on two distinct sets of skills: basic skills and concept skills (p. 93). Curriculum maps, as described by Heidi Hayes Jacobs (1997), provide the structure for identifying and planning for instruction in both the basic and concept skills areas.

In Danielson's view, planning for instruction in the basic skills would ensure the following:

- Each student is placed accurately on the learning continuum. The fact that students are 10 years old and in fifth grade does not mean all of them are ready to learn (or still need to learn) fifth-grade material. Accurate assessment to determine placement on the learning continuum facilitates continuous progress for students.
- Students are assigned to appropriate instructional groups based on their placement in the curriculum.
- Flexible structures permit the assignment of students to different instructional groups as their learning needs change.

Team planning for instruction in the concept skills requires teachers to:

- Organize curriculum around large themes to help students investigate major topics in depth and identify patterns or trends.
- Integrate basic skills throughout the curriculum. For example, the skills of expository writing learned in language arts can be applied to essay writing in science or social studies.
- Integrate critical reasoning skills throughout the curriculum. Such skills would involve classification, comparing and contrasting, pattern recognition, judgment, synthesis, and evaluation.

Differentiated instruction: The strategy/style connection. Carol Ann Tomlinson has written numerous books in which she identifies strategies for responding to the needs of all learners through differentiated instruction. In her address at the 2003 ASCD Annual Conference, she identified principles of quality of instruction that matter more than the strategies for differentiating instruction. The principles she identifies include:

- Commitment to growth, to helping students see themselves in a better light
- A belief in challenging all students and giving them a feeling of accomplishment
- A sense of community, where every student knows that he or she has something special to contribute
- A determination to create a solid curriculum, one formed by a clear sense of purpose
- A magnet-like relationship to assessment
- A belief that curriculum should offer all students "a way up, not a way out"

So much is now known about designing learning experiences that match instructional strategy with student learning style that differentiation to address student readiness, interest, and talents is no longer a mystery. A great deal of research and practical guidance is available to assist teachers in making the strategy/style connection.

The key to differentiation is the rotation of instructional strategies in order to address varying styles of learning and to challenge students to learn in a variety of ways. Flexible groupings allow students with similar learning styles or instructional needs to work together for periods of time. Whether students struggle or need an extra challenge, making the strategy/style connection allows instruction to be individualized. The differentiation challenge for educators resides in ensuring that they learn about the strategy/style connection, that they accurately

assess their students, and that they actually plan to incorporate them in their practice.

Staff development: The teacher/student learning connection. Staff development through participation in professional learning communities results in benefits that cannot be overstated. Teachers learn with and from each other through mutual exploration and action research aimed at bettering student achievement by improving instruction. This kind of staff development focuses on student knowledge and outcomes.

Collegial professional development, however, focuses on enhancing the professional skills of teachers. While students ultimately benefit, the goal of this kind of staff development is to increase teacher knowledge and instructional competence. The two kinds of staff development are distinct, but neither is superior to the other. They have different purposes and are equally important.

There is a wealth of advice pertaining to professional development. Marzano (2003) identifies key elements of lesson design. Wiggins and McTighe (1998) have developed an Understanding by Design template to "engage students in exploring and deepening their understanding of important ideas and the design of assessment to reveal the extent of their understandings" (p. 3). Howard Gardner speaks of multiple intelligences and how everyone is "smart" in his or her own way. The implications for instruction based on student aptitudes in various intelligences are huge. Eric Jensen (1998) and Patricia Wolfe (2001) are gurus of brain-based learning and give us guidance in using what is known about the brain to provide optimal instruction. Art Costa and Bena Kallick (2000) tell us about habits of the mind, while Silver and Strong (2003) speak of learning styles and provide a Learning Style Inventory that reveals learning preferences to consider when planning instruction.

The list of examples cited above, though not exhaustive by any means, is representative of the vast repertoire of skills, knowledge, and competencies required of teachers. Effective teachers have a wide array of strategies that they know how and when to use. A strong, focused program of staff development honors the complexity of the learning process and supports teachers in achieving their professional potential. Students ultimately benefit.

Learning: The instruction/assessment connection. Instruction and assessment are inextricably connected. There are varied forms of assessment, all of which are appropriate in specific circumstances. External assessment is represented by state, provincial, or district exams. School- or classroom-based assessment comes in a variety of forms ranging from paper and pencil tests through interviews and observation to authentic assessment tasks that require students to perform in a situation that approximates "real life." Rubrics are a relatively new addition to the assessment picture and can provide a rich source of information about both individual and collective student progress. Rubrics are written, agreed-upon criteria or guides by which student products or performances are judged. Different proficiency levels are identified, and the qualities of work exhibited at each level are clearly indicated. Rubric development provides a useful framework for discussions between teachers or between teachers and students about performance standards or benchmarks for achievement.

Mike Schmoker (1996) has identified three reasons to use rubric assessment, paraphrased below:

1. Rubrics clearly define good performance and show that it is achievable.
2. Rubrics provide precision and clarity about the evaluation criteria.
3. Rubrics take the mystery out of learning by informing students about how they will be evaluated. (p. 71)

Rubrics bring fairness to assessment by giving both students and teachers clear direction about the evaluation criteria. Student reflection about their own performance as well as goal setting for improvement are facilitated when rubrics are available. Rick Stiggins, director of the Assessment Training Institute in Portland, Oregon, has made the study of fair assessment practice a priority in his work. DuFour and Eaker (1998) quote the five standards for quality assessment practice identified by Stiggins and his associates:

> **Standard 1:** Quality assessment is built on clearly identified knowledge and skills that students are expected to master.
>
> **Standard 2:** Quality assessments are designed to provide teachers with the information they need to inform and improve their instructional practice.
>
> **Standard 3:** A quality assessment program will provide information that benefits teachers, students, parents, and the broader community. Teachers need information about the achievement of each of their students. Students need to know how their performance compares to the benchmarks. Parents need information about how their children are doing, and the community at large needs data on the collective effectiveness of its schools.

> **Standard 4:** Quality assessments provide enough information about enough students to allow conclusions to be drawn about overall student achievement.
>
> **Standard 5:** Quality assessments are designed, developed, and used in a way that minimizes factors that might interfere with the accuracy of the results. Such factors might include, among other things, poor test construction; assessment that is not aligned with the intended curriculum; test items that reflect racial, ethnic, or gender biases; or a testing environment that is not conducive to concentration. (p. 174)

We recognize that there is much concern about external standards testing. Our contention is that if schools combine clearly aligned curricula with differentiated instruction and quality assessment practices, results on external assessments will take care of themselves.

Area Four: Parent Involvement

Effective schools research identifies positive home-school relations as one of the seven correlates. Positive, proactive collaboration with parents and other significant adults who are integral members of the school community has a powerful impact on student achievement.

Marzano (2003) cites parent and community involvement as the third school-level factor contributing to student success. Success, he claims, "has to do with the extent to which parents (in particular) and the community at large (in general) are both supportive of and involved in a school" (p. 47). We have identified three different, yet equally important, functions for relationships that exist between schools and parents/community:

1. Communication and collaboration
2. Involvement with the school
3. Consultation

Communication and collaboration. Working together, teachers and parents can support each child's learning and development as an individual. Parents are a child's first teachers and, as such, are valuable partners for teachers. They have insights about their children's personalities and learning patterns that can help teachers get to know and understand those students better and more quickly. Teachers can also be valuable supporters for parents because they see children in different settings and can provide parents with information about where their support is needed for continued growth and learning. If parents are aware of what their children are learning at school, they can extend and reinforce it through activities at home. Effective communication is the key.

There are many ways in which schools can communicate with parents and caregivers. Newsletters, phone calls, e-mail messages, web pages, home visits, curriculum overviews, parent-teacher conferences, progress reports, and report cards are just a few methods of communication. Meet-the-teacher evenings and special parent information sessions provide other means of communicating. Consultation with parents, staff, and the community at large will identify preferred frequency and methods of communication for each school community.

Involvement with the school. Parents and members of the community at large offer a vast array of skills and abilities that can enhance a school's climate. Volunteers can provide support directly to the classroom through working with students individually or in small groups. They can also support teachers by

Six Roles for School-Home Interactions
(Epstein, 2001)

1. **Parenting**—Help all families establish home environments to support children as students.
2. **Communicating**—Design effective forms of school-to-home and home-to-school communications about school programs and children's progress.
3. **Volunteering**—Recruit and organize parent help and support.
4. **Learning at home**—Provide information and ideas to families about how to help students at home with homework and other curriculum-related activities, decisions, and planning.
5. **Decision-making**—Include parents in school decisions, developing parent leaders and representatives.
6. **Collaborating with community**—Identify and integrate resources and services from the community to strengthen school programs, family practices, and student learning and development.

assuming responsibility for such things as preparing curriculum support materials, displaying student work, and arranging field trips or special events. Parents themselves are often excellent resources for learning. They can contribute as speakers as well as facilitate community learning experiences through visits to places such as museums, factories, restaurants, and zoos. Community service opportunities for students provide another

avenue through which parents and other members of the community can contribute.

Another arena for involvement is the Home and School or Parent Advisory Council or the local PTA chapter. This participation can be enormously helpful through collaboration on such things as lunch or breakfast programs, safety patrols, and fundraising to support school activities, projects, and resources. Such participation not only lightens the load for staff, but also supports the school's culture and supplements its resource base.

Consultation. Parents and other interested members of the broader community have much to contribute to the articulation of the school's values, vision, and purpose statements. Broad-based consultation that includes all stakeholders (staff, students, parents, interested members of the broader community) is imperative if a school is to serve its community effectively.

A consultative process is very useful when reviewing school structures, policies, and practices. It is important that parents have the opportunity to help identify what is important for the school their children attend. Their feedback and input on how the school functions relative to its stated values and vision can provide invaluable critical evidence for the planning for school and student success process.

While the school staff has the primary responsibility for reflection on critical evidence that leads to goal-setting and subsequent creation of the school plan, parents have an important role to play in monitoring and supporting its implementation. The School Success Management Team, which is established in the implementation phase of the Planning for School and Student Success Program, provides a mechanism for involving parents. This involvement enables parents to support the staff and communicate with the broader community as the plan is being implemented.

When parents and members of the broader community are included in the life of the school in respectful and authentic ways, positive interpersonal relationships and lines of communication can be developed that will support all stakeholders when inevitable conflicts arise. Attention to building strength in this one correlate results in a positive impact on the other six. Involving parents is a high-yield strategy.

Summary

At this point in the process, we can find guidance in the words of author and physician Oliver Wendell Holmes:

> I find the great thing in this world is not so much where we stand, as in what direction we are moving: To reach the port of heaven, we must sail sometimes with the wind and sometimes against it—but we must sail, and not drift, nor lie at anchor.

Members of professional learning communities collaborate with each other to identify high-yield strategies for the achievement of goals. Planning to improve necessitates action. As action is taken, support and monitoring are required. Chapter 10 focuses on this implementation process.

Chapter 10

Implement

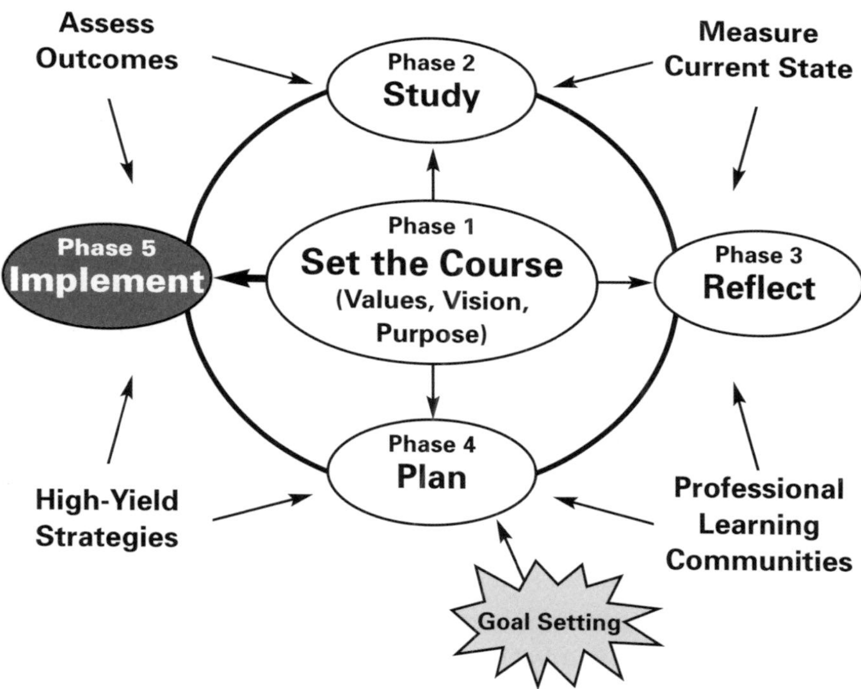

The Planning for School and Student Success Process results in the establishment of goals and plans for improvement. The planned changes become reality in the implementation phase of the process. At this point the real impact of change and the accompanying expectation of accountability will be felt. Lezotte and McKee (2002) tell us that "change is simple . . . it's just not easy!" (p. 199). We concur.

Getting the Amoeba Across the Road

Wayne Hulley refers to the school improvement process as "getting the amoeba across the road." Webster's dictionary defines amoebas as tiny one-celled animals that lack permanent cell organs and live in water. They do not have a supporting structure and tend to want to separate as they move. We see school improvement work as being very much like an amoeba in that it is neither static nor predictable. It is constantly evolving and changing, responding to new information and incorporating new learning as plans to improve are developed and implemented. We can extend this analogy further by pointing out that the Planning for School and Student Success Process is a morphological structure that supports the amoeba as it moves. It morphs as the work of reculturing is carried out. To successfully deal with the amoeba, staff members will have to be committed to making the journey and they will require a lot of support, encouragement, and monitoring if they are to stay the course. Shared values and vision will guide the process as momentum gathers and challenges inevitably present themselves.

Progress in some areas can be made quickly; however, deep, meaningful change is likely to take time. This is particularly true if the change involves shifting the school culture—and almost any significant change will. To prevent discouragement and abandonment, divide big-picture areas designated for improvement into smaller, more discrete parts. In that way, work can be prioritized and approached in a way that feels more manageable.

Conditions for Facilitating Change

(Adapted from John Kotter, 1996)

- **Establish a sense of urgency.** Regular meetings with the School Success Management Team provide the impetus for regular review of actions being taken by the PLCs and of the results they are seeing. These meetings make tangible the expectation of action and the resulting sense of urgency.
- **Create a guiding coalition.** Involving key stakeholders on the team creates an important guiding coalition.
- **Communicate the change vision.** One of the most important roles of the team is communication with the school community about what is planned and how things are proceeding.
- **Empower broad-based action.** Broad representation on the team encourages all stakeholders to support the improvement initiative. When students, parents, and central office personnel understand the goals, they can find ways to offer their support in achieving them.
- **Consolidate gains and produce more change.** Regular meetings between PLCs and the team will result in consolidation of gains and will allow next steps to be determined.
- **Anchor new approaches in the culture.** One of the main roles of the team is to prepare an annual summary of progress made by the school and the students.

In chapter 8, "Plan," we identified a number of challenges facing professional learning communities: procrastination (the "planning to plan" trap), resistance (clinging to the status quo), and over-reaching (trying to do too much too soon). If the planning phase of the process has been successfully navigated, the staff will be ready to begin the implementation phase. Guided by a shared purpose, armed with critical evidence, and confident in the goals that have been set, the staff working in professional learning community teams will have chosen high-yield strategies to help them reach their goals. The preceding phases of the Planning for School and Student Success Process will have provided the support necessary for the "amoeba" to continue its journey toward success.

This chapter provides guidance on the School Success Management Team, creating the formal plan for action, the implementation process, and the how and why of the monitoring process.

The School Success Management Team

The School Success Management Team was discussed in chapter 4's consideration of the issue of leadership when a school plans to improve. The purpose of this team is to support and monitor implementation of the school plan. Communication is a primary function of this team. It meets regularly, perhaps bimonthly, with representatives from each of the professional learning communities, who will report on their goals, their work, the progress their PLCs are making, and their requests for support. The School Success Management Team is also responsible for communicating the planning process to the groups they represent and for preparing a summative report on the planning process at the end of each school year. The report's primary purpose is to inform the staff and community about progress toward the goals identified in the school plan. Many schools prepare an overview version of the school plan

report for distribution to the community. The School Success Management Team can also be the vehicle for making mandatory reports to district, state, provincial, or federal authorities.

Creating the Formal Plan for Action

The formal school plan is composed of the goals set by the various professional learning communities in the school. Among other things, this plan will describe the character and competence goals, the plans to achieve them, and the means of monitoring progress toward them.

An effective school plan will focus on areas that are important to the school and the district. While each school's plan will be unique to its context, the various goals of different schools in a district must be aligned with those of the district as well as those of the province or state. A number of plan formats are available. Regardless of the format, each school's plan must be completed in a way that addresses the accountability issues faced by educators today. The plan must be professional in its structure and should give anyone who reads it a sense that the school has a clear grasp of the future it is trying to create.

School plans could include the following five sections:

1. School profile
2. The planning process
3. Values, vision, and purpose statements
4. School planning goals
5. Structures and strategies to be implemented

We have provided a number of questions for each section below. The answers to these questions will guide a school staff as it develops the plan.

School Profile

- How can the student population be described in specific ways? For example, should data be disaggregated by gender, grade enrollments, ethnic or racial group, exceptionalities, language spoken in home, socioeconomic status, or family structure?
- How can the staff members be described in specific ways: by experience level, training, or role (i.e., classroom teachers, specialists, teaching assistants, administration, support staff)?
- How can the school describe the grade levels and special programs present in the school?

The Planning Process

- Who was involved?
- What process was followed?
- How were decisions made?
- How often were meetings held?

Values, Vision, and Purpose Statements

- What does the staff care about most?
- What does the staff hope to achieve?
- Why do we exist? What matters most to students, parents, staff, and the broader community?

School Planning Goals

This section is a compilation of the goals identified by the entire staff and the professional learning community groups. The questions will reflect both character and competence goals as we have described them.

- How are the school goals aligned with those of the district and province or state?
- Are the goals clearly stated, and do they identify an expected outcome? Using the SMART goals format would ensure that they are specific and strategic, measurable, attainable, results-based, and time-bound. If goals do not include a statement of expected outcome, they are not specific enough.

Structures and Strategies to Be Implemented

- Which high-yield strategies will be used?
- How will they be implemented?
- Who will implement them?
- What will the indicators of success be for each goal?
- Which data sources will be used to collect critical evidence about progress toward the goals?
- How often will progress be monitored?
- How will it be communicated?
- How will the need for adjustments, if any are required, be determined?
- How will additional supports that are required be determined and provided?

The Implementation Process

Throughout this book, we have emphasized the importance of total staff involvement in the Planning for School and Student Success Process. If this has been arranged, there will be no surprises when the formal school plan is drafted. We acknowledge that not all staff will be committed and involved to the same extent; however, we believe that it is imperative that all be given the opportunity to have input into the plan so that, in the final analysis, they know what is included, how it got there, and what it means for them.

The school plan reflects the shared values, vision, and purpose statements that were developed for the school. Involvement in their creation may not necessarily result in commitment from all members of the staff, but it will certainly go a long way toward conveying expectations. Communication of the school plan through members of the School Success Management Team makes an important statement about the school's priorities that will be appreciated by the various stake-holding groups in the school community.

The implementation process itself can be expected to have some ups and downs. This is the phase in which the real impact of planning for improvement is felt. This is where the actual change process is realized, and where educators are most vulnerable to the lure of past practice and "comfortable" structures. DuFour and Eaker (1998) tell us that "schools have demonstrated time and again that it is much easier to initiate change than to sustain it to fruition. Until changes become so entrenched that they represent part of the 'way we do things around here,' they are extremely fragile and subject to regression" (p. 105). According to DuFour and Eaker, "in most organizations, what gets monitored, gets done" (p. 106). Monitoring the implementation of the school plan is an important function of the School Success Management Team.

The Monitoring Process

The ability of the School Success Management Team to fulfill its mandate completely depends upon the kind of relationship it

establishes with the school's staff. If a relationship is built that is based on trust and trustworthiness, the staff will view the team as a helpful and supportive partner on the school improvement journey. If, on the other hand, members of the team are perceived as having "power over" the rest of the staff, the chances for productive working relationships will be greatly diminished.

There should be no question in the minds of anyone involved that the job of the School Success Management Team is to support the implementation of the school plan—not to supervise or evaluate members of the staff.

The team's monitoring function includes observing the implementation process, asking the right questions, and searching for ways to support the staff in their work. Through regular meetings with representatives from each of the PLCs, the team will hear about the work being done, progress being made, and challenges being encountered. The focus of conversations between staff and the team should revolve around the following issues:

- Alignment between stated goals and the school's shared statements of values, vision, and purpose
- Progress being made on plan implementation
  - What do we hope to achieve?
  - What are we doing to achieve those goals?
  - How do we know if we are making a difference?
  - What are we doing if we are not making a difference?

- Implementation successes and challenges
  - What aspects of the plan are working well?
  - How can we celebrate the progress being made?
  - Do staff members have enough collaboration and planning time?
  - Are present structures and practices in place at the school conducive to goal attainment?
  - Are required materials available to support the implementation process?
  - Are the goals articulated properly, or do they need to be revised for increased feasibility?

The team also assumes a consulting role as it connects with its various stakeholder groups to track implementation of the school plan and monitor pertinent issues. It is imperative that the team listens to the feedback from all groups and adjusts the plan as needed to stay on course for achieving the goals that have been set.

Recognition, Encouragement, and Celebration

We can expect staff members to become weary from time to time as they move forward. Change is hard work and serious business. Many new initiatives will be successful on the first attempt. Some, however, will not. Teachers may become overwhelmed and lose confidence as they try new things. Some of the new ventures will not live up to expectations; in fact, some may be complete failures. Fullan (2001) identifies this inevitable stage of struggle and setbacks in the change process as the "implementation dip."

The role of the administration and School Success Management Team now intensifies. At this point, teachers need unfailing support to "keep the faith" in order to learn from the efforts that did not work. They need to know that the risks they have taken in trying something new are recognized and that their competence will not be judged because things did not work the first time. Support for this kind of action research will result in teacher commitment to finding what works best in helping students achieve. Over an extended period, this supportive attitude toward teachers and their practice will shift the culture of the school from one of teacher isolation to one of collaboration. The outcome will be enhanced learning and achievement by all.

Most educators are excellent at encouraging students and celebrating their successes. They do less well when it comes to celebrating their own success and that of their colleagues. The importance of celebration cannot be overstated. Regardless of their age or occupation, people appreciate recognition for effort, achievement, talent, and contribution. For teachers who are refocusing their professional efforts to maximize student achievement, recognition and celebration may rekindle commitment and enthusiasm when the going gets rough—as it is sure to do. Celebration helps to remind the staff of the "big picture" in the plan, thus reinforcing the shared values, vision, and purpose of the school. Through celebrating the accomplishment of planning milestones and the achievement of stated goals, teachers who have been actively involved receive well-deserved recognition and the skeptics in the group will receive another clear message about the power of collaboration and the importance of their commitment to the plan.

Summary

The development of the school plan report is the final task of the School Success Management Team because it is the culmination of their work. Its creation provides the school with the opportunity to reflect on the successes and challenges encountered as the implementation process unfolded. While we do not recommend waiting until the annual report is being written to recognize the excellent school improvement work being done by staff, we do recognize it as an ideal time to collectively celebrate and highlight accomplishments and successes. It is also a time to recognize staff members who have taken leadership roles in the process. The creation of the school plan marks the starting point for the next step in the cycle of continuous improvement and sets the stage for the Planning for School and Student Success Process to begin again.

Chapter 11

Creating the Culture for Change

The Importance of Alignment

In chapter 2, we stressed the importance of alignment to support the Planning for School and Student Success Process. School districts provide powerful support for the process when they consistently communicate the message that improvement in student achievement is the critical issue and that schools and teachers will be supported in their efforts to improve. At the school level, principals provide tangible support for the process when they create structures and processes that honor teachers as the true change agents, since they are the ones who interact directly with students. In a culture of support and encouragement, teachers can feel confident about implementing new instructional strategies without fear of negative consequences if the strategies do not work as planned.

The Importance of Leadership

The School and Student Success Process is a school improvement model that can support the reculturing of a school. The model's cyclical structure is meant to encourage deeper, richer reflection and planning with each year that goes by. Reculturing is not immediate. In fact, it may take up to 3 years. Reculturing involves change, and change can be a turbulent process, characterized by intense emotion. When emotions are aroused, leadership becomes more important than ever before.

The complexity and chaotic nature of the change process pose interesting dilemmas for those in leadership positions. Ambiguity reigns supreme and the lure of returning to old ways is seductive. Leaders who are facilitating change need highly refined emotional intelligence skills in order to know how and when to press on, change direction, or back off. Those guiding a reculturing process need a sophisticated understanding of the concept of "shared leadership," along with the skills to cultivate this kind of leadership at all levels.

Fullan (2001) speaks of the issues facing education today as being "rife with paradoxes and dilemmas" (p. 2). Leaders with strength of character and strong competence are required to deal with these issues, because there are no quick and easy answers. Leaders who demonstrate character exhibit the habits of effective people as described by Stephen Covey (1989). They are proactive and take responsibility for their choices. They are aligned to a personal mission and spend time on the things that matter most. In their work with groups, they strive to reach win/win agreements by listening for understanding. They strive to build the culture and commitment to school and student success that will result in synergistic working relationships among members of their staffs. Competence is shown through the management function of the leadership role. Character and competence combine to result in a powerful set of skills and attitudes

that couple genuine caring for people and a deep understanding of how to support, inspire, and motivate them in planning for school and student success.

Personal Traits of Effective Leaders

Energy	Character
Enthusiasm	Competence
Hopefulness	(Covey, 1989)
(Fullan, 2001)	

Fullan conceives of five components of leadership that are interdependent forces for change. In the school context, they can be described in this way:

1. **The presence of moral purpose**—acting in order to have a positive impact on the lives of students, staff, parents, and society as a whole.
2. **Understanding of the change process**—Fullan identifies six guidelines for leaders to consider when dealing with the process of change:
    - The goal is not to innovate the most.
    - It is not enough to have the best ideas.
    - Appreciate early difficulties of trying something new—expect an "implementation dip."
    - Redefine resistance encountered as a potential positive force.
    - Reculturing is the name of the game.
    - Never a checklist, always complexity.

3. **Relationships**—if they improve, things get better. If they remain the same or get worse, ground is lost.
4. **Knowledge creation and sharing**—examined information from within the school and from the broader community becomes knowledge that can be used for school improvement. Fullan is quick to say that knowledge-building is dependent upon moral purpose, understanding of the change process, and positive relationships.
5. **Coherence making**—the process of identifying patterns, structures, and ideas that are worthy of embedding in the culture of the school. In Fullan's words, "complexity keeps people on the edge of chaos. It is important to be on that edge because that is where creativity resides, but anarchy lurks there too" (p. 6). Effective leaders know that some level of ambiguity is conducive to creativity. They also recognize that there comes a time to put an end to the disequilibrium and consolidate the learning that has occurred.

Robert Marzano (2002) asserts that effective leadership is a necessary and critical condition for school improvement efforts at the school, teacher, and student levels. In fact, he takes the position that "leadership could be considered the single most important aspect of effective school reform" (p. 172). The term "instructional leader" has been used in that regard for a long time; however, what it really means has remained ambiguous and unclear. Marzano's research indicates that "leadership has a strong relationship with (among other things):

- The extent to which a school has a clear mission and goals
- The overall climate of the school and the climate in individual classrooms

- The attitudes of teachers
- The classroom practices of teachers
- The organization of curriculum and instruction
- Students' opportunity to learn (p. 172)

Findings of the McRel Study of Leadership

(Marzano and associates cited in Waters, Marzano, and McNulty, 2003, p. 221)

1. **Leadership matters.** Effective school leadership leads to greater student achievement.
2. **Effective leadership can be empirically defined.** There are 21 key leadership responsibilities that are significantly correlated with higher student achievement.
3. **Effective leaders not only know what to do, but when, how, and why to do it.** This is the essence of balanced leadership.

The Importance of Principal Leadership

There is a lot of evidence to support the notion that leadership is best distributed throughout the organization for maximum impact. Leadership shared is also leadership multiplied. We feel strongly, however, that the effectiveness of efforts to share leadership and the success of the planning process are directly dependent upon the vision, beliefs, skills, and support offered by the "formal" leaders in the school, particularly the principal. Although power and responsibility should ideally be shared, the significance of the principal's role must not be underestimated. We are convinced that without the principal's direct, visible involvement in the school planning process, the best intentions and efforts of other members of the staff will not reach their potential. Direct and visible involvement means that a principal must take a stand about the importance of school improvement. Principals will share their vision for their schools, ask important questions, facilitate research and collaboration, and keep the process moving forward. When principals tangibly illustrate their support for all that is entailed in school planning, they create the conditions and mindsets that will allow reculturing to occur.

According to DuFour and Eaker (1998), effective principals lead through shared values and vision. They involve staff in decision-making processes and empower individuals to act. Information, training, and parameters are provided to guide staff in making good decisions within a "loose-tight" leadership style. Principals will be "loose on the strategies that teachers use to advance vision and values, but they will be 'passionately tight' on the fact that values and vision must be adhered to" (p. 187). Effective principals establish credibility by modeling behavior that reflects school values and vision. In the words of Stephen Covey (1989), they "walk their talk." They are results-oriented and work with staff to set measurable goals, identify desired outcomes, and monitor them continually.

Schmoker (2002), in describing the leadership provided by Rick DuFour at Adlai Stevenson High School, concludes that "leadership consists of method, not magic" (p. 19). At Stevenson, teachers were routinely given leadership responsibilities, though they were not given free rein. DuFour provided clear boundaries within which teachers could work creatively and autonomously.

Clear parameters, obligations, and deadlines, and the expectation of concrete accomplishments characterized the work environment for teachers at Stevenson.

Empowerment does not mean neglect or abandonment.

Passionate commitment to the realization of the stated vision ought to fuel all conversations, all decisions, and all commitments to action in schools that plan to improve. Schmoker (2002) believes that without data, vision cannot exist. It is his opinion that data are what substantiate the vision. Data can demonstrate that "unprecedented levels of achievement are within our reach" (p. 20). Teachers will be willing to try new strategies and structures if there is evidence that they will be effective. Under strong, uncompromising leadership the right questions will be asked with the right frequency. In Schmoker's words, "leadership is defined and actualized through constant, gentle confrontation. It shows us where we are and guides us to where we want to be" (p. 21).

Understanding the Accountability Issue

Accountability is a word often used in the current context of school improvement conversations. It is a word that has the potential to cause great anxiety if it is not understood. The notion of accountability is just one of many changes that teachers and administrators have had to grapple with in the past few years. It is probably the most misunderstood, and therefore most threatening, term of all. To deal effectively with the term "accountability," educators must first come to grips with the emotional impact it has on them, individually and collectively.

It is our belief that, because of the complexity of schools and the learning process, collaboration, teamwork, and mutual support are the things that will result in a collective confidence about being held "accountable" for student achievement. To be accountable, educators must work together to accept responsibility for providing quality instruction that results in improved student achievement.

Principals are accountable for everything that happens in their school. They must focus on working with staff to ensure that learning is happening for all students. Principals are not responsible for what goes on in individual classrooms because, typically, they do not have teaching responsibilities. They are, however, accountable for what goes on in their schools.

Teachers are responsible for classroom instruction and student outcomes. They work to enhance their students' success. Principals work with teachers for the same reason. If they are to instruct students appropriately, teachers require knowledge and skill to be able to differentiate instruction and address student learning needs. To be effective in their supervisory role with teachers, principals require knowledge about differentiation with students as well as with their staff.

Zmuda, Kuklas, and Kline (2004) take the position that "collective accountability" is the way to achieve a vision for the school and a collective confidence about being able to make a difference. Accountability, in their view, must extend from the formal leadership to temporary leaders who emerge during the change process, then, ultimately, to all staff members. When staff members see themselves as collectively and individually responsible for enhanced learning and achievement for all students, they have accepted their role in being accountable. This thinking requires

a cultural shift that necessitates working within the context of professional learning communities predicated on relationships that are characterized by mutual respect and trust. The importance of strong leadership to facilitating this change cannot be overstated—nor must the challenges be underestimated.

Shared Leadership

Linda Lambert and associates (1997) see school leadership as a broad concept that is separated from person, role, and behaviors. Leadership, in their opinion, needs to be embedded in the school culture with all members sharing responsibility for a shared purpose. Terrence Deal (1999) supports this notion. Successful schools, he explains, "have leadership emanating from many people—leadership that maintains and supports learning for all students as well as learning for staff" (p. xiii). The key notion in this view is that leadership is about learning together in a culture that shares common values, vision, and purpose. The key activity is collaboration.

According to Lambert and associates (1997), this view of leadership requires a redistribution of power and authority such that superintendents and principals adjust their view of "authority" and teachers develop the competencies to enhance personal and collective power as well as informal authority (pp. 122–143). Patterson and Patterson (2004) believe that long-term teachers have more opportunity than do short-term principals to positively affect the culture of a school. They point out that teacher leadership may be either formal (i.e., a department head) or informal. In their opinion, those who provide informal leadership "earn their place as culture leaders through three sources of influence: credibility, expertise and relationships" (p. 75).

Lezotte (1991) identifies the shift to teacher as leader as a shift from a first to a second generation of leadership. Improving schools usually begins with the first generation of the "instructional leadership" correlate; however, sustained improvement and a shift in culture require that a school move to the second generation. The first generation must be embedded in the culture before the second generation can be achieved.

The first generation. In this phase of leadership, the principal acts as an instructional leader persistently communicating the school's values, vision, and purpose to all affected parties. In the first generation, standards for instructional leadership focus primarily on the principal of the school, who understands and applies the characteristics of instructional effectiveness in the management of the instructional program.

The second generation. In the second generation, the concept of instructional leadership is expanded to view leadership as a dispersed concept that includes all staff, especially the teachers. This shift recognizes that a principal cannot be the only leader in an organization as complex as a school. To be effective, the leadership focus must evolve so that the creation of a "community of shared values" becomes a priority. The mission/purpose remains critical because it serves to give the community a shared sense of "magnetic north," an identification of what this school community cares most about.

The role of the principal in the second generation changes to that of leader of leaders, rather than leader of followers. In specific terms, this means that the principal will have to rely on coaching skills and function as a partner and cheerleader. The principal will continue to focus on instruction and will spend much time supporting teachers in achieving better results. At

this stage, the principal functions as a "guide on the side" in working with staff. This broader concept of leadership recognizes what teachers have known and good schools have capitalized on since the beginning of time: expertise is generally distributed among many, not concentrated in a single person.

The school improvement process is like a parade with the principal's role varying as it moves along its route. Sometimes principals will need to be at the front, with the baton, leading the parade. At other times they will need to beat the drum to coordinate the band and keep the rhythm. Occasionally they will have to walk behind the horses and clean up the pavement! The true joy comes, however, when they can stand on the curb and cheer as the parade goes by.

"Collective accountability," as identified by Zmuda, Kuklas, and Kline (2004), implies that through collaboration, teachers and administrators will assume leadership roles depending upon who is most qualified. When leadership becomes a distributed property among all staff, teachers can guide and support one another through the change process. Those in formal leadership positions need to find ways to provide teachers with the time they need to collaborate with each other and to provide the professional development they need in order to assume leadership roles. By viewing all teachers as potential leaders, administrators adopt an "equal opportunity" mindset with the goal of finding ways to support teachers individually in acquiring the skills that will enhance both their teaching and their leadership abilities. In this way, administrators can differentiate their supervisory practice to provide the most appropriate support for each teacher.

> "Shared leadership recognizes the concepts of shared fate and shared accountability. . . . It requires that leaders know each other and that all members of the leader-follower team have a reasonable assessment of the strengths, weaknesses, and tendencies of each of their peers. . . . As a group, the shared decision-making team is less like an orchestra, where the conductor is always in charge, and more like a jazz band, where leadership is passed around among the players depending on what the music demands at the moment and who feels most moved by the spirit to express that music."
>
> —Schlecty (2001, p. 178)

Developing a culture of shared leadership is not without its challenges. Marzano (2003) discovered in his research that the egalitarian culture of schools in which all teachers are considered equal, regardless of their expertise or performance, makes this vision of shared leadership difficult to achieve. He quotes Friedkin and Slater (1994) to describe this phenomenon: "Teachers' physical isolation in pursuing instructional activities and their norms of professional autonomy, privacy and equity serve to inhibit the emergence of strong informal leaders from their ranks" (p. 174). This presents a dilemma to those in formal leadership positions and challenges them to find ways to coach and promote teacher leadership in their schools.

The importance of developing a culture of shared leadership is underscored by the fact that the formal leadership of a school often changes fairly regularly. While the advantage of new leadership rests in new ideas, new approaches, and new enthusiasm, the disadvantage is that innovations run the risk of dying with the departure of the formal leader. Another disadvantage rests in the fact that some staff, realizing that this principal is probably only here for a little while, may not engage in school improvement initiatives, opting instead to "wait until this one goes away." If change is to become embedded in a school's culture, responsibility for creating it must ultimately reside with the entire staff. This is possible only when leadership is shared within the staff. A history of shared leadership in a school is the single most important factor in ensuring that change is sustained after the formal leader has left.

The Importance of Sustainability

Is it easy to sustain momentum in the school planning process? It certainly is not. Ensuring sustainability is hard work. It requires a school to stay the course on improvement initiatives beyond the end of a year. Changes in staff; a new administration; new expectations of the district, state, or province; frustration with lack of progress; satisfaction with the progress made; or the pull of old ways, can all make it difficult to sustain continuous improvement.

When we designed the Planning for School and Student Success Process, we thought carefully about this issue. Building teams, sharing leadership, establishing clear goals, focusing on results, introducing high-yield strategies, and celebrating progress are intended to create a school culture focused on success. We recommend that the planning cycle be initiated during the spring term so that the plan is in place for the next school year. In that way, new staff members can be introduced to the plan and opportunities for their contributions can be discussed. A review of the previous year's plan and the results achieved will help them understand that they are joining a staff that values planning to improve and holds high expectations for student success. Their involvement with existing professional learning communities will further support their transition into the new culture.

Maintaining consistency at the principal level is one of the greatest challenges to sustaining momentum and embedding change in school culture. School districts require flexibility in the placement of principals to meet system needs. Principals who successfully demonstrate leadership that balances high expectations with professional support are valuable to the district and are often considered for transfer or promotion.

We believe the Planning for School and Student Success Process supports sustainability when changes occur in formal management positions. For an incoming principal, the school plan is a powerful introduction to the school. As part of the transition process, the outgoing principal can share his or her understanding of the school culture by reviewing the values, vision, and purpose statements. The goals and critical evidence that supported their creation can be explored. Plans that have been implemented and the critical evidence of their impact can be examined. New principals will look at the plan with fresh eyes, and will be in a position to ask important questions and contribute new ideas. They can begin the new school year already positioned to work at enhancing the culture, supporting the changes already made, and finding ways to sustain the momentum. The principal is not so much an agent of change,

as previously thought. In this respect, the role of the principal is to be a supporter of a culture of change.

Leaders Develop Sustainability . . .

- By committing to and protecting deep learning in their schools;
- By trying to ensure that improvements last over time, especially after they have gone;
- By distributing leadership and responsibility to others;
- By considering the impact of their leadership on the schools and communities around them;
- By sustaining themselves so that they can persist with their vision and avoid burning out;
- By promoting and perpetuating diverse approaches to reform rather than standardized prescriptions for teaching and learning; and
- By engaging actively with their environments

—Hargreaves and Fink (2004, p. 13)

The story of Sacred Heart Community School is a story of, among other things, sustainability through the creation of a culture that supports change and continuous improvement. At the outset, Loretta Tetrault knew she had to plunge in to get the process started. As staff worked and learned together, leadership was distributed among them to the extent that when Rob Currie took over as principal, the staff took him by the hand and said, "This is how we do things around here." Loretta had left a lasting legacy. The changes she began had become embedded in the culture of the school so that when she retired, the staff assumed responsibility for ensuring that the changes survived. Rob's challenge was to sustain and build upon the momentum. By the end of his second year there, Rob and the staff had been successful in that regard. The culture of continuous improvement was being sustained. Sacred Heart provides inspiration for others who are engaged in planning for school and student success that can be sustained over time.

Summary

Creating a culture for change requires the ability to deal with ambiguity, anxiety, and conflict. It is difficult, but not impossible. Meaningful and shared statements of values, vision, and purpose provide a compelling catalyst for change; however, without leaders with a passion for schools and learning, the changes that are envisioned are not likely to be realized.

Leadership is about change and influence. It is about "taking people from where they are now to where they need to be. The best way to get people to venture into the unknown terrain is to make it desirable by taking them there in their imaginations" (Tichy, 2002, p. 16). The Planning for School and Student Success Process is a proven pathway to the creation of a culture for change.

Chapter 12

Building on Success: Continuous Improvement

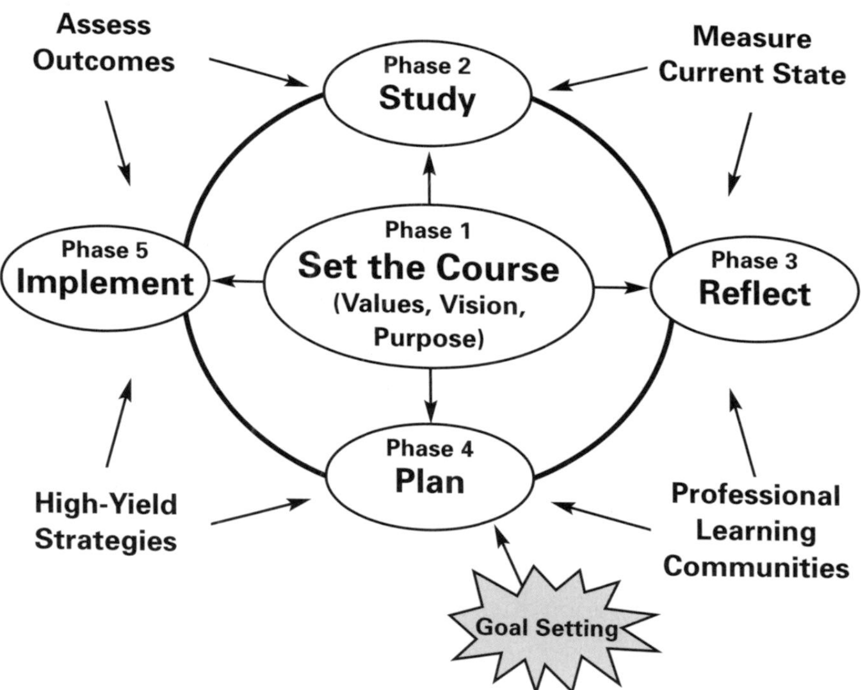

As much as we have tried to present the Planning for School and Student Success Process as a model to guide a school's school improvement efforts, we are aware that any suggestion of its being linear, predictable, or tidy is completely misguiding. Any school improvement process that results in meaningful, lasting change is full of ambiguity and challenge. While guidelines can be provided and lessons can be learned from other schools, the improvement process in every school will be unique. Demographics and existing cultures have a large impact on the process. Staff characteristics and the quality of leadership also have a large impact. The planning process will be uneven and messy. There will be many turns in the road and mountains to be climbed. Passionate commitment combined with tenacity and perseverance on the part of everybody involved are the things that will, in the end, see the process through to fruition. The key concept is improvement. The key activity is collaboration. The outcome is hope.

The wonderful thing about school planning is that it never ends! It is cyclical and every year there is another opportunity to review the goals and build on the work of the previous year. The annual report on the school plan is summative and identifies, among other things, the goals for improvement along with the high-yield strategies that will be used to work on them and the tools and methods that will help to assess progress. The final report also includes outcomes of the work done that year and evidence of the extent to which goals were met, as illustrated by assessment of the performance indicators. The summative school plan report identifies not only areas to be celebrated but also areas that still need attention. It provides the starting point for the planning process in the year to come.

The First Year

The first year of the Planning for School and Student Success Process will involve a tremendous amount of work. There will be numerous challenges as staff members strive to understand the importance of the process and the vital role they play in it. Time will no doubt be a factor, given the requirement for collaboration and teamwork that is inherent in the plan. Outreach to various stakeholders also takes time and may feel risky until relationships are built and common values, vision, and purpose are established. The good news, however, is that, once completed, the work of the first year will provide the foundation and impetus for subsequent years. The course will have been set for the creation of a stronger-than-ever Harbor of Hope.

While the first year of the process does require a lot of time and energy from all involved, it can also be an exhilarating experience. When staff and other members of the school community commit to a common set of beliefs and come together to create their dream of a better place, a synergy results that will sustain them in their work. At the outset, they will be fuelled by the novelty of the process and the excitement of charting a new course. It is an inspiring time. We must also recognize, however, that over time, energy levels will start to drop and excitement will wane as the inevitable challenges to successful improvement present themselves. Starting the change process is simple compared to what it takes to sustain it.

Five elements will help a school sustain its change process:

1. Relationships
2. Hope
3. Leadership
4. Reculturing
5. Collaboration

Relationships

Throughout this book, we have talked about the importance of solid relationships based on trust and trustworthiness. In our opinion, the quality of relationships has an impact on every interaction with every person on every issue encountered in the planning process. We have also emphasized in many different ways the necessity of shared values, vision, and purpose. When those have been clearly articulated, the ground rules for interpersonal relationships as well as educational goals and practice are laid.

Hope

Hope has been defined as "unwarranted optimism in the face of seemingly insurmountable odds." It is not a vague feel-good concept. Hope is what happens when people cling tenaciously to the belief that they can make a difference when, in fact, it would be easier to doubt and give up. Students in schools that are Harbors of Hope know that they are surrounded by people who care passionately about them and are committed to doing whatever it takes to help them be successful. "Learning for All—Whatever It Takes" is a reality in a Harbor of Hope school.

Leadership

The depth in which we have discussed the topic of leadership emphasizes the importance we place on it. Effective leadership that is distributed throughout the staff is the key to making change happen in the first place and to making it stick in the long run. The long run is of particular importance—change must be sustainable. For the sake of students and staff, we can no longer allow improvement initiatives to be started and then lost when principals move on. Collective accountability means that all staff, as a collective body, and all staff as individuals, must assume

responsibility for identifying the areas that need improvement, collaborating to plan for addressing them, and working to achieve the desired results.

Reculturing

The Planning for School and Student Success Process is not a fill-in-the-blank activity in which a school staff completes the five phases, files the plan, and returns to the "real" work of teaching. If planning is approached with this mindset, then a school has slipped into what we have referred to throughout this book as "planning to plan," and the outcome will be the intent to change without any real change. The Planning for School and Student Success Process involves fundamental change as a process of school reculturing.

Collaboration: Teachers Are the Key

The most essential element of this reculturing is the activity of collaboration, and teachers are the key to its success. Collaboration brings teachers to the center of the change process. The Planning for School and Student Success Process is intended to change the way teachers think and behave. Teachers matter. They are very important people in very important roles. Acknowledgement of this fundamental truth, along with supportive structures and practices, is what will result in a plan for improvement that enhances learning outcomes for all students.

In professional learning communities that operate from a foundation of shared values, vision, and purpose and are passionate about providing hope for every student, teachers collaborate to provide excellent teaching for all. Teachers who are supported in working this way will see themselves as "school teachers" and not only as "classroom teachers." They will feel responsible for the learning and success of all students in the school. When this happens, the school culture that has been created is one in which teachers "plan to improve." It is teachers, not the plan, that make the difference in a school.

> I have come to a frightening conclusion. I am the decisive element in the classroom. It is my personal approach that creates the climate. It is my daily mood that makes the weather. As a teacher I possess tremendous power to make a child's life miserable or joyous. I can be a tool of torture or an instrument of inspiration. I can humiliate or humor, hurt or heal. In all situations, it is my response that decides whether a crisis will be escalated or de-escalated, and a child humanized or de-humanized.
>
> —Haim Ginot (1995, p. 178)

Better Together: Final Thoughts

We have written this book to help educators create schools that become Harbors of Hope for all members of the school community. Although we are not researchers, we have between us over 70 years of experience working in and with schools. What we have shared with you is what we have found works in schools that make a difference for all students. We call these schools Harbors of Hope. They are places where staff is motivated and positive, where principals are proud and passionate, where all students experience success, and where community support is high. We have found that educational research over

the past 35 years supports what we have discovered through practical experience.

We cannot direct the winds
but we can adjust our sails.

The Planning for School and Student Success Process results in excellent teaching and a school culture that ensures "Learning for All—Whatever It Takes." It is the process, not the product in the form of a school plan, that is important. We hope you will find it useful on your journey of school improvement. We have not promised that the process will be simple. We do feel confident, however, in promising that it will be both exciting and challenging. When schools improve for the sake of students, the journey is worth the effort.

Part 3

Appendix

Appendix

Thirteen Brain-Activating Strategies

One of the many steps taken by Sacred Heart Community School in Regina, Saskatchewan, toward becoming a Harbors of Hope school was the creation of a "Brain-Activating Oasis" that would focus on individual learning. The staff identified 13 brain-activating strategies and techniques to be used in the oasis. This appendix provides a brief summary of these 13 strategies.

1. Changing From Teaching to "Activating Brains"

The staff determined to change their view of their role as teachers. They redefined themselves as "inventors of work worth doing" and used an integrated curriculum approach to make this a reality.

2. Incidental Learning: The Little Things Are the Big Things

The Sacred Heart staff worked from the premises that much of learning is incidental, and that when people experience feelings of safety and belonging, they are more able to learn. The staff recognized that school environment and atmosphere have a huge impact on students' ability to learn, and they made it their goal to create a school that is friendly and inviting.

3. Stimulating Environment

At Sacred Heart, most of the classrooms do not look like traditional classrooms. There are few desks to be found. Students work at a variety of tables, on couches, on cushions, or in easy chairs. Plants help to bring nature inside. Fish, pets, and other items of interest add to the environment and afford more opportunities for learning. Teachers are often found working with small groups in a variety of locations. The unique class combinations provide stress-free settings where multi-age teamwork can flourish and negative peer pressure is minimized. An integrated thematic approach to instruction is used, allowing for large blocks of dedicated time. Often several classes work on the same theme so that students can learn from interactions beyond their classroom and grouping can be more flexible.

4. Hallway Huddles

The Sacred Heart staff believes that teachers and students benefit from opportunities to work and learn together. Hallway huddles are opportunities for students to meet with the neighboring classrooms and engage in collaborative activities related to the theme being studied. Huddles consist of students, often of several ages, working together and with adults on learning activities. Groupings are fluid and respond to student interest and need.

5. Learning States

According to Jensen (1996), learning requires an appropriate "state," and a person's state affects both thought processes and physiology. Optimal states of curiosity, anticipation, suspense,

low to moderate (but never high) anxiety or stress, challenge, and temporary confusion are required if learning is to occur. The best learning occurs when there is a flow from one state to another. All learning is state-dependent. The staff at Sacred Heart has become expert at using a variety of strategies to help students achieve their optimal states for learning and skill development.

6. Music

Jensen's research illustrates that music can be used to charge and energize the brain. Certain kinds of music set the tone for learning, other kinds promote a feeling of celebration, while still others stimulate creativity or accelerate learning. Music can set the tone at the beginning and end of the school day and can become a comforting part of a predictable routine. Music plays a variety of different roles every day at Sacred Heart School. The use of music also provides an opportunity to expose the students to music they would not normally hear.

7. Brain Breaks

Brain research has illustrated that dominance between the right and left sides of the brain alternates approximately every 90 minutes. Regular "brain breaks" throughout the school day at Sacred Heart provide an opportunity for cross-lateral activities where the right and left hemispheres of the brain interact with each other. These breaks last for 60 seconds or less and result in refreshed, energized people with enhanced ability to learn. When students are given flexibility in how they learn, this natural cycle can be accommodated. It is not uncommon at Sacred Heart to hear students, especially the older ones, say that they need to take a brain break before they continue with their work.

8. Real Math

The Sacred Heart staff is committed to providing meaningful learning activities by connecting them to each student's reality. Since mathematics was difficult for many students, the staff collaborated to create "real-life" activities for students to pursue while learning mathematics. The senior teachers at Sacred Heart collaborated with each other to design an innovative math program for their students. Program outcomes are aligned with the curriculum, and teaching strategies are aligned with everyday life.

In this program, students earn "Sacred Heart money" for doing their job, which is attending school. They each have a bank account and they learn to develop a budget that will sustain them from payday to payday. They pay rent for their working space at the school as well as for other everyday school expenses. Savings plans and interest rates, risky and conservative investment plans, and the intricacies of borrowing are all part of the program. The students can earn bonus money for homework, outstanding improvement, or exemplary effort. They lose money when they arrive late, skip school, or break the school code of conduct. They learn to write checks and to understand the consequences of a bounced check. They become acquainted with automated teller use, credit card use, and related activities. Some students have even experienced the hardship of bankruptcy.

Students work together to problem-solve, apply for different jobs, write resumes, prepare for and go through interviews, and take upgrading to improve their "salaries" if they are not satisfied with their current income. The excitement around "payday" is a joy to behold.

9. Eye Patterns and Thinking

According to Jensen (1996), thinking involves accessing or creating "modal representations" that fall into four categories: visual, aural, emotional, and other. Mind, body, and feelings are never separated in the learning process. Cognitive activity occurring in one hemisphere triggers eye movement in the opposite hemisphere. At Sacred Heart, students are taught about eye patterns and are trained to use them to enhance their thinking ability. They also use them as cues in their interactions with students.

10. Daily Oral Language

Determined to build on existing oral language skills, the staff introduced a program called Daily Oral Language at all grade levels as a means of stimulating thinking, strengthening oral communication skills, building community, and supporting the acquisition of reading skills. Oral language activities include quick exercises that address a variety of language skills. They are light, easy, fun to solve, and generally end in a cooperative learning activity. Students really enjoy them, and there has been a positive impact on test scores in this area as a result.

11. Mind Mapping/Concept Webbing

Knowing the benefits of multiple-path learning and globalization as a learning technique, graphic organizers like mind mapping or concept webbing are taught to Sacred Heart students at all levels. These kinds of organizers assist with organization, understanding, and recall as well as with note taking and information gathering. Graphic organizers help students connect what they are learning to prior learning and can make new material more relevant.

12. Assessment

The staff of Sacred Heart has collaborated to develop assessment rubrics in key areas at all grade levels in order to provide continuous instruction and growth for all students. They believe that students need to know what they are expected to learn as well as how they will be assessed. Portfolios are also used as a means of involving students in their own assessment and as a means of demonstrating growth.

13. Our Catholic Faith

Sacred Heart School is part of the Regina Catholic School District. Staff members believe that their shared beliefs enhance their ability to influence learning through the sense of community and service they have developed. The entire school body meets several times each week to sing and pray, and to celebrate the school and each other. They affirm that they are a Catholic school and have consciously worked to create a hope-filled faith environment that permeates all that they do.

References

Barth, R. (1991). Restructuring schools. *Phi Delta Kappan, 73*(2), 125–129.

Blanchard, K., & Muchnick, M. (2003). *The leadership pill.* New York: Simon & Schuster.

Bridges, W. (1991). *Managing transitions: Making the most of change.* Don Mills, Ontario: Addison-Wesley.

Conzemius, A., & O'Neill, J. (2002). *The handbook for SMART school teams.* Bloomington, IN: National Educational Service.

Costa, A. L., & Kallick, B. (2000). *Activating and engaging habits of mind.* Alexandria, VA: Association for Supervision and Curriculum Development.

Covey, S. R. (1989). *The seven habits of highly effective people.* New York: Simon & Schuster.

Danielson, C. (2002). *Enhancing student achievement: A framework for school improvement.* Alexandria, VA: Association for Supervision and Curriculum Development.

Deal, T. (1985). The symbolism of effective schools. *The Elementary School Journal, 85*(5), 601–620.

Deal, T. E., & Peterson, K. D. (1999). *Shaping school culture: The heart of leadership.* San Francisco: Jossey-Bass.

Deming, W. E. (1989). *The new economics for industry, government, and education.* Cambridge, MA: Massachusetts Institute of Technology, Center for Advanced Engineering Study.

Drucker, P. (1996). *Managing for the future: The 1990s and beyond.* New York: Truman Talley Books.

DuFour, R. (2004). What is a "professional learning community"? *Educational Leadership, 61*(8), 6–11.

DuFour, R., & Eaker, R. (1998). *Professional learning communities at work.* Bloomington, IN: National Educational Service.

Eaker, R., DuFour, R., & Burnette, R. (2002). *Getting started: Reculturing schools to become professional learning communities.* Bloomington, IN: National Educational Service.

Edmonds, R. R. (1982). Programs of school improvement: An overview. *Educational Leadership, 40*(3), 8–11.

Effective Schools League (2004). Posting on the "Views and Information" section by Loretta Tetreault. http://www.effectiveschools.com/

Epstein, J. L. (2001). *School, family and community partnership: Preparing educators and improving schools.* Boulder, CO: Westview Press.

Fullan, M. (1993). *Change forces: Probing the depths of educational reform.* London: Falmer Press.

Fullan, M. (1997). Emotion and hope: Constructive concepts for complex times. In A. Hargreaves (Ed.), *Rethinking educational change with heart and mind.* Alexandria, VA: Association for Supervision and Curriculum Development.

Fullan, M. (2001). *Leading in a culture of change.* San Francisco: Jossey-Bass.

Fullan, M., Bertani, A., & Quinn, J. (2004). New lessons for districtwide reform. *Educational Leadership, 61*(7), 42–46.

Gardner, H. (1993). *Frames of mind: The theory of multiple intelligences.* New York: Basic Books.

Gardner, H. (1999). *The disciplined mind: Beyond facts and standardized tests, the K-12 education that every child deserves.* New York: Simon & Schuster.

Ginot, H. (1995). *Teacher and child: A book for parents and teachers.* Princeton, NJ: Scribner Press.

Glickman, C. D. (1993). *Renewing America's schools: A guide for school-based action*. San Francisco: Jossey-Bass.

Goleman, D. (1995). *Emotional intelligence*. New York: Bantam Books.

Goleman, D. (1998). *Working with emotional intelligence*. New York: Bantam Books.

Hargreaves, A., & Fink, D. (2004). The seven principles of sustainable leadership. *Educational Leadership, 61*(7), 8–13.

Jacobs, H. H. (1997). *Mapping the big picture: Integrating curriculum and assessment K-12*. Alexandria, VA: Association for Supervision and Curriculum Development.

Jensen, E. (1998). *Teaching with the brain in mind*. Alexandria, VA: Association for Supervision and Curriculum Development.

Kotter, J. (1996). *Leading change*. Boston: Harvard Business School Press.

Lambert, L. (1998). *Building leadership capacity in schools*. Alexandria, VA: Association for Supervision and Curriculum Development.

Lambert, L., Kent, K., Richert, A. E., Collay, M., Dietz, M., et al. (1997). *Who will save our schools? Teachers as constructivist leaders*. Thousand Oaks, CA: Corwin Press.

Lezotte, L., & McKee, K. M. (2002). *Assembly required: A continuous school improvement system*. Okemos, MI: Effective Schools Products, Ltd.

Lezotte, L. W. (1991). *Correlates of effective schools: The first and second generation*. Okemos, MI: Effective Schools Products, Ltd.

Lezotte, L. W. (1997). *Learning for all*. Okemos, MI: Effective Schools Products, Ltd.

Louis, K. S., Kruse, S., & Raywid, M. A. (1996). Putting teachers at the center of reform. *NASSP Bulletin, 80*(580), 9–21.

Marzano, R. J. (2003). *What works in schools: Translating research into action*. Alexandria, VA: Association for Supervision and Curriculum Development.

Marzano et al. (2003). As cited on p. 221 in Waters, T., Marzano, R. J., & McNulty, B. (2003). *Balanced leadership: What 30 years of research tells us about the effect of leadership on student achievement.* Aurora, CO: Mid-Continent Research for Education and Learning.

McTighe, J., & Wiggins, G. (1998). *Understanding by design.* Alexandria, VA: Association for Supervision and Curriculum Development.

Newmann, F., & Wehlage, G. (1995). *Successful school restructuring: A report to the public and educators by the Center for Restructuring Schools.* Madison, WI: University of Wisconsin.

Newmann, F. M. (1998). How secondary schools contribute to academic success. In *The adolescent years: Social influences and educational challenges* (pp. 88–108). Chicago: University of Chicago Press.

Patterson, J., & Patterson, J. (2004). Sharing the lead. *Educational Leadership, 61*(7), 74–78.

Reeves, D. B. (2004). *Accountability for learning.* Alexandria, VA: Association for Supervision and Curriculum Development.

Rosenholtz, S. J. (1991). *Teacher's workplace: The social organization of schools.* New York: Teachers College Press.

Ross, R. B. (1994). The five whys. In P. Senge et al., *The fifth discipline fieldbook.* New York: Doubleday.

Schlecty, P. C. (2001). *Shaking up the school house: How to support and sustain educational innovation.* San Francisco, CA: Jossey-Bass.

Schmoker, M. (1996). *Results: The key to continuous school improvement.* Alexandria, VA: Association for Supervision and Curriculum Development.

Schmoker, M. (2000). The results we want. *Educational Leadership, 57*(5), 62–65.

Schmoker, M. (2001). *The results fieldbook.* Alexandria, VA: Association for Supervision and Curriculum Development.

Senge, P. (1990). *The fifth discipline: The art and practice of the learning organization.* New York: Doubleday Currency.

Sergiovanni, T. (2000). *The lifeworld of leadership*. San Francisco: Jossey-Bass.

Sergiovanni, T. (2004). Building a community of hope. *Educational Leadership*, *61*(8), 33–37.

Silver, H. E., & Strong, R. W. (2003). *Learning style inventory*. Ho-Ho-Kus, NJ: Thoughtful Education Press.

Spence, C. (2002). *On time! On task! On a mission!* Halifax, Nova Scotia: Fernwood Publishing.

Spillane, J. P., Halverson, R., & Drummond, J. B. (2001). Investigating school leadership practice: A distributed perspective. *Educational Researcher*, *30*(3), 23–28.

Stiggins, R., Webb, L. D., Lange, J., McGregor, S., & Cotton, S. (1997). *Multiple assessment of student progress*. Reston, VA: National Association of Secondary School Principals.

Tichy, N. M. (2002). *The leadership engine*. New York: HarperCollins Publishers, Inc.

Tomlinson, C. A. (2003). *Fulfilling the promise of the differentiated classroom: Strategies and tools for responsive teaching*. Alexandria, VA: Association for Supervision and Curriculum Development.

Waters, T., Marzano, R. J., & McNulty, B. (2003). *Balanced leadership: What 30 years of research tells us about the effect of leadership on student achievement*. Aurora, CO: Mid-Continent Research for Education and Learning.

Wolfe, P. (2001). *Brain matters: Translating research into classroom practice*. Alexandria, VA: Association for Supervision and Curriculum Development.

Zmuda, A., Kuklus, R., & Kline, E. (2004). *Transforming schools: Creating a culture of continuous improvement*. Alexandria, VA: Association for Supervision and Curriculum Development.

Make the Most of Your Professional Development Investment

Let National Educational Service schedule time for you and your staff with leading practitioners in the areas of:

- **Professional Learning Communities** with Richard DuFour, Robert Eaker, Rebecca DuFour, and associates
- **Effective Schools** with associates of Larry Lezotte
- **Assessment for Learning** with Rick Stiggins and associates
- **Crisis Management and Response** with Cheri Lovre
- **Discipline With Dignity** with Richard Curwin and Allen Mendler
- **SMART School Teams** with Jan O'Neill and Anne Conzemius
- **PASSport to Success** (parental involvement) with Vickie Burt
- **Peacemakers** (violence prevention) with Jeremy Shapiro

Additional presentations are available in the following areas:

- At-Risk Youth Issues
- Bullying Prevention/Teasing and Harassment
- Team Building and Collaborative Teams
- Data Collection and Analysis
- Embracing Diversity
- Literacy Development
- Motivating Techniques for Staff and Students

BB181

NEED MORE COPIES OR ADDITIONAL RESOURCES ON THIS TOPIC?

Need more copies of this book? Want your own copy? Need additional resources on this topic? If so, you can order additional materials by using this form or by calling us toll free at (800) 733-6786 or (812) 336-7700. Or you can order by FAX at (812) 336-7790, or visit our website at www.nesonline.com.

Title	Price*	Qty	Total
Harbors of Hope: The Planning for School and Student Success Process	$ 21.95		
Learning for All	24.00		
Assembly Required: A Continuous School Improvement System	34.00		
Whatever It Takes: How PLCs Respond When Kids Don't Learn	24.95		
Getting Started: Reculturing Schools to Become PLCs	19.95		
Professional Learning Communities at Work (video set)	495.00		
Professional Learning Communities at Work (book)	24.95		
How to Develop a PLC: Passion and Persistence	24.95		
Through New Eyes: Examining the Culture of Your School	174.95		
The Handbook for SMART School Teams	54.95		
SUBTOTAL			
SHIPPING Continental U.S.: Please add 6% of order total. Outside continental U.S.: Please add 8% of order total.			
HANDLING Continental U.S.: Please add $4. Outside continental U.S.: Please add $6.			
TOTAL (U.S. funds)			

*Price subject to change without notice.

❑ Check enclosed ❑ Purchase order enclosed
❑ Money order ❑ VISA, MasterCard, Discover, or American Express (circle one)

Credit Card No.________________________ Exp. Date__________
Cardholder Signature ________________________

SHIP TO:

First Name________________ Last Name________________
Position ________________________
Institution Name________________________
Address________________________
City________________ State______ ZIP__________
Phone________________ FAX________________
E-mail ________________________

304 W. Kirkwood Avenue
Bloomington, IN 47404-5132
(812) 336-7700 • (800) 733-6786 (toll-free number)
FAX (812) 336-7790
e-mail: nes@nesonline.com • www.nesonline.com